Daniel Carter Beard

Moonblight and Six Feet of Romance

Daniel Carter Beard

Moonblight and Six Feet of Romance

ISBN/EAN: 9783743305168

Manufactured in Europe, USA, Canada, Australia, Japa

Cover: Foto ©ninafisch / pixelio.de

Manufactured and distributed by brebook publishing software (www.brebook.com)

Daniel Carter Beard

Moonblight and Six Feet of Romance

Foreword.

The purest saint who ever lived has had thoughts as evil, perhaps, as any that ever entered the mind of the most abandoned; but these thoughts, like vultures that fly through the summer sky, leave no trace behind in the crystal mental atmosphere of the saint.

We are responsible only for such thoughts as we, by our own choice, detain and harbor in our minds. Our responsibility begins when we interrupt the flight of the vulture, and tempt it to alight by the offer of food. The evil becomes our own when the vulture becomes domesticated.

Many birds-of-paradise, glittering as with the splendor caught from the inmost heaven, fly through the clouded minds of the most depraved; but if there is no home nor food offered them, they also disappear and leave no trace of what has passed through the mind. The good comes only with the domestication of the birds-of-paradise.

Through the mental heavens of the author, two birds, "Moonblight" and "Six Feet of Romance," have flown, and he is responsible for them only so far as he has sheltered and fed them. They came from a land beyond his ken, and would, like birds of passage, have flown on, and left nothing to tell of their existence had not their strange notes attracted his attention and interest. One twittered a light song, and the cry of the other was the warning scream of a mother bird. Although neither may possess the brilliant plumage of the bird-of-paradise, yet the author trusts and believes that neither may be classed with the vulture.

Who can deny that the old-fashioned superstition that certain men sell themselves to the devil is a literal truth of to-day? His Satanic Majesty uses them as overseers on his earthly plantations; and for that proud office, and the emoluments that go with it, these men have bartered their souls.

If a word or sentence in this book should cause a single slave-driver to transmute the baser earthly coin into the fine gold of love and the silver of truth, the author will know he has not been deceived in the nature of the birds that have visited him.

If you place a valuable picture with its face against the wall, and leave it in darkness, the beautiful tints will fade, the white turn yellow, the flesh-tints green, and the whole become dim, indistinct, and ugly in color; but if this same picture be placed in God's clear sunshine, the colors will return to all their original brightness, enriched and deepened by their temporary exile in the darkness.

There is a wall called Vested Rights, which prevents nature's sun from shining on our fellow-men; but, thank God! good workmen are busy at its foundation; it is already undermined and *must* fall. Then, and then only, will the poor tramp, the beggar, and the white slave begin to show the true color of their manhood.

List of Illustrations.

	PAGE
Frontispiece.	
Initial Letter (Chapter I.)	17
"I Could not Light My Pipe"	19
To Let	30
"So My Chain's Makin' Me a Slave, See?"	34
Seeing Things as They Really Are	37
Initial Letter (Chapter II.)	42
The Witch	44
"I Wish I Could See Things as They Really Are"	47
"The Cursed Pigskin-Covered Book"	54
Initial Letter (Chapter III.)	59
"I Had Attended a Meeting of Mine Owners"	60
"A Red-Mouthed Wolf with White Fangs"	66
"True Expression of the Inner Mr. White"	67
Initial Letter (Chapter IV.)	72
A Type of the Modern So-Called Christian	75
Prejudice	81
"Now, Mister, What Does That Mean?"	83
"Now, Mister, What Does That Mean?"	85
"What Does This Mean, Mister, Say?"	87
One of the Customers	90
A Forgotten Well	92
Initial Letter (Chapter V.)	95
"The Moon is All Right"	96
Prof. Follium	97
Clint Butts, My Superintendent	104
The Old Continental	117
"The Old White-Faced Moon Saw This"	120
Initial Letter (Chapter VI.)	128
A Sketch From Nature	130

	PAGE
Its Application	131
"I Am a Firm Believer in Gnomes," etc.	134, 135
Initial Letter (Chapter VII.)	146
Ah, the Hardship, Privation, and Suffering of a Strike!	147
The Law Locks up What a Loving God Has Created for His Children	148, 149
"The People in the Cities Read of These Strikes, and Grumble at the Inconvenience It Causes Them"	151
Modern Civilization	154
The Editor	156
Two Distracted Mothers Were Sobbing, etc.	159
What Abe Lincoln Did Say	163
"Force Begets Force"	167
Initial Letter (Chapter VIII.)	174
The Old Paths	182
A Red-Faced Old Club-Man	184
New Paths	189
The Woman's War-Club	193
The End	197
Initial Letter (Six Feet of Romance)	201
The Great Log Fire	203
An Old-Fashioned Foot-Stove	204
"A Hand Reached Out of the Haze"	206
"There Were Two Feet Side by Side"	208
A Pair of Yellow-Topped Boots	210
I Have Always Regarded These Boots with a Feeling Akin to Awe	212
Self-Conscious Boots	214
Two Hands Reached Down Simultaneously, as if to Take the Stove	216
"Only to Immediately Appear"	218
Tail-Piece	221

MOONBLIGHT.

BISMAL, dismal, dismal! Rain in torrents, rain in drizzles, rain in mist!

Big rolling clouds of smoke and mist, low-hanging gray clouds, fast-driving, ragged aërial tramps of the sky!

Howls of angry winds, moans of melancholy winds, sobs and sighs of weary winds!

Such was the history of the day after my arrival at the straggling, dirty mining town in Pennsylvania where my business had called me.

My steam yacht was at Port Jefferson, Long Island, out of commission for the winter. I had parted with my jolly comrades only two days ago, but it seemed like ages.

The American House, where I was domiciled, is a small frame building, the counterpart of hundreds of others of the same name scattered all over Uncle Sam's broad domain.

I had drummed upon the battered piano in the second-floor parlor ; I had lounged in the dreary apartment which served as barroom and office ; I had examined the prints of gorgeous and not over-modest females posing in lithographic ink as advertisements for sundry cigarette firms ; I had thrown myself upon the gaudy bedquilt that covered the couch where I had slept the night before, but the cotton-seed oil in which my eggs were fried, or the greenish-yellow saleratus biscuit, or their combination, had given me heart-burn and indigestion.

For the twentieth time I took my pipe from its satin-lined case. Even this appeared to share the general depression : the beautiful amber mouthpiece seemed a trifle more cloudy, the richly colored brown bowl, in which I took so much pride, was covered with a thin mist that dulled the warm tints.

I wiped off the pipe, filled it, and after wasting breath and endangering my soul by meaningless epithets applied to the country matches that would not ignite, I broke a whole section of them off the block. They stood up like a file of soldiers, just as regular and just as stupid. One brisk rub across my trouser's leg, a smudge, a smell of brimstone, and then a flame. I could not light my pipe: it would not draw.

I threw pipe and tobacco on top of my sole-leather trunk, and went to the window. It was covered with mist. With my hand I wiped clear a spot large enough to look through.

A dismal, straggling street met my view—a discouraged-looking street, with a preponderance of mud and saloons. Trudging along in a disheartened sort of manner came a file of black-faced, black-handed, dirty, wet

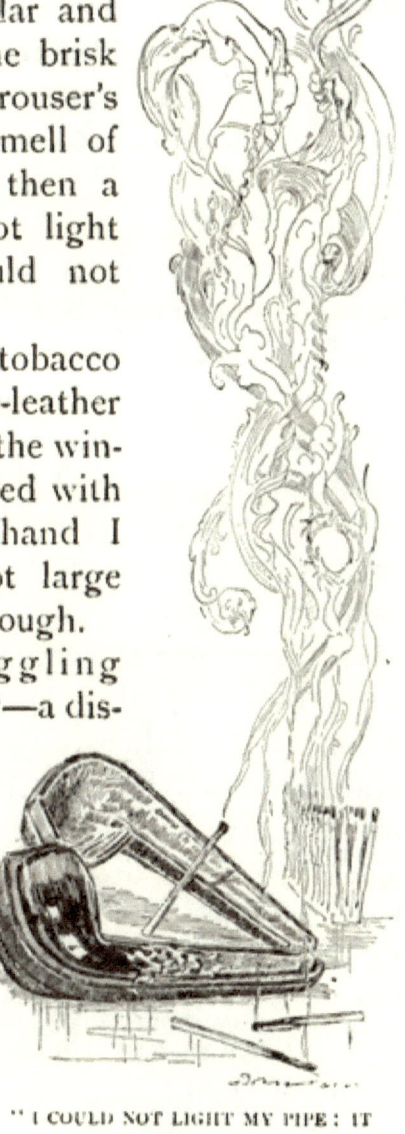

"I COULD NOT LIGHT MY PIPE: IT WOULD NOT DRAW."

men and boys, each with a clanking dinner-pail Somehow or other the clanking pails reminded me of clanking chains, while the coal-dust on their faces rendered it impossible to tell whether the real color of the skins was black or white. The next instant a picture that I had seen somewhere of a gang of black slaves rose before me. I turned from the window in despair, and my eyes fell upon a shelf of books.

The landlord had informed me, the night before, when I registered, that there was no room vacant, but that he would put me in a room usually occupied by a regular boarder, who was at present temporarily absent; and this was the room.

In the corner stood a fowling-piece in its leathern case; alongside of it were several fishing-rods in their drab cloth covers. These and other articles of a like nature, hanging in the corner, under and around the book-shelves, I now noticed for the first time, and they gave me the only thrill of pleasure that I had experienced since my arrival the night before.

The presence of the rod and gun brought on an independent camp-life feeling. I picked up my pipe, and with a broomstraw removed the obstruction in the stem, and refilled it with aromatic tobacco. I shook the ashes from the prim, cylindrical stove, and put on more coal; then, selecting a glowing coal from the ashes, by skillful juggling, and by dint of keeping it moving from one hand to the other, as I had learned in camp to do, I guided it successfully to my pipe's bowl, and soon had a beautiful light with no taint of sulphur matches. Then, throwing a wrap over a rocking-chair, and lighting the coal-oil lamp, I fixed myself comfortably before the stove with a book.

Although my life since leaving Ohio had been one of pleasure and idleness, I had a strong inherited attachment for books, and I never saw a strange volume without experiencing an almost irresistible desire to know what was contained between its covers. Many social engagements have I broken by becoming absorbed in some quaint volume found in one of the numerous bookstands that abound on Ann, Nassau, and Fulton streets.

Evidently the regular boarder was a man with tastes similar to mine; for although the books on his shelves were not numerous, they were all quaint and such as I would select; but most of them were strangers to me. If his room had been in the city, where the money-value of such treasures is known, he most probably would have been compelled to keep them under lock and key. Here, however, their safety lay in the ignorance of the people, who probably would never be tempted even to examine such an antiquated, dilapidated-looking collection.

However that might be, there the books were in plain sight, now that the lamp was lighted and my attention attracted to them, and formed a sight to make a book-fancier's heart beat and his fingers itch.

In selecting the volume I was to read, I instinctively chose one of the most worn and ancient in appearance. The fire brightened, the sound of dripping rain and sobbing wind was lost to my ear, the biscuit and cotton-seed oil at last gave up their struggle with a healthy digestion, my pipe never tasted sweeter, and the rude jests and brutal oaths of the bar-room loungers below became but a subdued murmur.

There came a sound louder than the moaning winds; it grew in intensity, now louder still, now deafening, but I heeded it not. It was the supper-gong. Buried deep in the interesting work of spelling out the black-lettered words and admiring the brilliantly illuminated initials of the parchment leaves of the book, the indigestible supper had no charms for me.

"Dreams and Moonblight" is the title of the work. The book was evidently written after printing was invented and when black-letter was falling into disuse; yet the monkish author, with the reverence for tradition born of his life and the teachings of his church, had painfully written the book by hand, letter for letter, giving the same amount of thought and skill to the artistic handling of his pen as he did to the literary composition. The golden illuminated initials were exquisitely done and of the mediæval Celtic style of ornament.

I had indeed discovered a triumph of the book-making art, nor did its contents lack interest. It contained quaint old bits of philosophy and a knowledge of nature that must have placed the author far in advance of the scholars of his time. His reasoning was marked by a clear and concise method, and, in spite of the antique manner of expression, was not difficult to understand. At least, so it appeared to me. As I turned over the stained yellow vellum leaves, a more than usually curious, ornate, and intricate initial met my eye; it evidently denoted an important chapter. I began to read, and as I read the black-letter became more familiar, the initials were unnoticed, my interest as a collector was absorbed in my interest as a bookworm.

After a long apology for daring to think that everything in nature was not a succession of miracles of the prestidigitator's sort, but only law-abiding events, the old monk began his essay as follows:

ERE I set before you good reader many good godly truths as I think it good and necessary and my bounden dutye to aquaynt you with.

Accordinge to the sayinge of Sainct Augustine: as there is, neyther shall be, any sinne unpunished euen so shall there not be any good deede unrewarded.

Although good reader I write in playne termes, and not so playnely as truly, concerning the laws of dreams, meaning honestly to all men and wish them as much good as mync owne harte.

With stout audacity and bolde words I give my thoughts.

When a healthy holsome man has hadde great cheere with much goode meate and bread and yet agaync much more meat and bread and fell to his mammerings and mouched apace, and agayne, because of his greate hunger or hoggishness, has taken more cheer, it be not wise for him to seek his couche.

For when he has plucked off his jerkin, untrussed him and removed his hosen and got him to bedde, he will oft times have untoward and wild visions and by the mass I wist not but he do sodanly wake.

Agayne there be certyne persons who by reason of weakness or sickness have blond that goeth but softly with not passing haste, when they sleep and these persons are likewise troubled with melencoyle fantasies and pevish ougly dreams.

If for ensample I dream that our most holy and reverened brother Awefeld comes to me in yerksome attyre and this glymmerynge fantasie with grete sword letes dryve with sodden force at me and I move not for lack of power to stepe but wake, with much dread and in grete fright. I cry out roll over and the fear departs hence and vanishes awaye with the visions it conjured up.

The author then proceeds to explain that persons suffering from "moonblight" are all those who are unable to distinguish their dreams from the realities of life. He showed how, in the "ensample" given above, if the author had not known after wakening, that his dream was not real, he would, at first sight of the harmless brother "Awefeld," have fled in great terror, or, worse still, have attacked the inoffensive subject of his nightmare with the first deadly weapon he could lay his hands on, and think he was only fighting to save his own life.

I had read thus far, and was thinking what a reasonable theory this was, when, before my mind's eye rose that cursed picture of a gang of black slaves with clanking chains that I had seen in the dirty wet street outside. It did not at first occur to me that the sight of black slaves in a Pennsylvania town was at all unusual, and I was only annoyed that my thoughts should revert to such unpleasant subjects; but when I realized the improbability and absurdity of negro slaves being in the streets of any town in the United States, twenty-five years after Abraham Lincoln had signed a document *freeing them all*, and when I thought of what the strange book said of the mooncalf that confounded his dreams with realities, I was alarmed.

"God 'ield the moonling!" I exclaimed as I flung the beautiful book upon the floor and hastily leaped from my chair.

Like a mendicant at the doorway of the mind, Fear ever stands begging for mental food and shelter. If alms are constantly and emphatically denied, the importunities of the mendicant become fainter and fainter until they are inaudible and we are unconscious of the pauper's presence. But food makes Fear a lusty beggar, whose strength and impudence are in direct proportion to the amount of nourishment he receives; and if but once he gains an entrance to the house of the mind, like a burly tramp, he will wreck the edifice and evict the tenants whose hospitality he has accepted.

It has not been my custom to extend any hospitality to Fear, and I have never been considered a coward; yet the horrible thought that my reason was leaving me I had never before faced, and the bare idea made my heart stand still; cold chills ran in waves down my spine, and the hair on the nape of my neck rose like that on the back of a frightened dog. I felt as though some horrible thing, vague and shadowy, was hovering over me, shutting off both air and light. My only thought was of escape—escape from myself! With a stifled cry I fled down the stairs to the smoky bar-room below.

The room was filled with rough men, drinking, swearing, and telling rude, pointless stories. No one noticed my agitation, nor in fact did my sudden appearance attract attention, which was a relief to my worried mind and made it easy for me to invite the crowd to the bar. I invited all of them, and they came up, but looked at me askance. With assumed abandon I seated myself upon the counter, and told all the stories I knew, and sang the jolliest "shanty" (chanty) songs, but the chorus was weak, and one by one the company I had thrust myself upon deserted, until at last the drowsy bar-keeper was the only companion left to me. My money and my powers of entertaining, that I had so often used with success aboard my yacht, did not prove attractive enough to secure me a handful of men to make a night of it with. However, I had in a measure regained my composure, and my native pluck helped in my need, while the thought of what my old comrades would say, if they saw me lose courage over a fit of indigestion, set me on my feet again. After helping the bar-keeper close up, I returned to my room. Before I could seat myself there was a knock at my unclosed door, and, looking around, I saw Sam, the bar-keeper, whom I had just left.

"Come in," I said, not for politeness' sake, but with the hope that he would do so, "Come in, Sam, and have a smoke!"

"Thanks," said Sam; "I thought I would drop in a minute to tell you that it's no use your trying to make friends with them fellers," jerking his thumb in a manner that indicated the bar-room, "for they's onter yer and know that you're one of the mine owners."

"Sit down, Sam," said I, in a cordial manner—cordial, because I liked Sam, and was in hopes he would sit down.

Sam seated himself, but declined to smoke, and as an apology said he never had learned how to use tobacco.

"Now, Sam," said I, "what's the matter with those men? I am not an aristocrat, I am only a man, just the same as they are, maybe a little better educated and dressed in finer cloth, but they have the same opportunities that my father had to gather wealth, for he worked as a day laborer, as a farm hand, and as a flatboat-man on the Ohio and Mississippi Rivers."

"Hold on, Mister!" said Sam. "Not so fast!" The sleepy bar-keeper brightened up,

and his eyes snapped as he repeated, "Not so fast, Mister! You're way off, clean off your base. Do you suppose that you would have the same chance as your old man did if you had no money ready made for you? Not by a long shot! When your dad and mine were young men, the land was not all owned by a few men; there was plenty of room West, and plenty of work."

"Bosh!" said I. "There is plenty of work yet; and as for the West, there is plenty of room there—acres and acres of land. I tell you such talk is all humbug!"

Sam's face changed; he smiled and winked at me in a knowing manner, and started to leave.

"Hold on, Sam; don't go yet," said I, dreading to be left alone more than I feared his bar-room arguments.

Sam reseated himself, and turning the conversation said, "Did you ever see me drink?"

"Come to think about it, no," I answered.

"Or smoke?"

"You have just declined."

"Do you think I am fond of tending counter in a gin-mill?"

"Can't say, Sam, as I ever thought of it."

"Well, I'm not!" said he in a decided tone. "I sometimes think I would rather be in hell; and I can give you the straight tip that I ain't far from it, either, when I stand behind the bar! Why don't I leave? Because I'm a *slave*."

Slave! The word brought up that cursed picture again.

"Nonsense!" said I, trying to drive the vision away.

"Ain't I?" replied Sam, in a fierce and sullen tone. "Look here! You're a land-owner and I am not. Now, somebody owns all the land, and as I own none of it, and you and I are all thet's present at this yere mass-meeting, you might as well represent der hull gang of landlords and I der hull gang of landless *slaves*."

"Don't call them that, Sam. I don't like to hear it."

"I won't; but I'll prove to you that they are. Here," he said—suddenly bringing to view from the pocket of his sack-coat one of those wonderful chains carved out of a single piece of wood and yet with separate links, and a ball inside a cube at the end, that we sometimes see exhibited as the work of prisoners, executed to while away the tedious hours of their captivity—"Here," he said, "is something I have made myself with a jack-knife."

"It is very curiously and skillfully made," I said, examining it with interest.

"Is it mine?"

"Yes," I assented, "I suppose it is if you haven't given it away or sold it to any one."

"I ain't giving nothing away," said Sam. "It ain't wuth to sell. All the same, I cut it outn a solid cedar stick and just fur argement's sake, we'll 'low it's wuth money and stands for my labor. Make believe, while we're about it, thet this yere is all I got—see?—all I got; and thet's not so far from true, as the first part of the make believe. Now, bein' as I'm too poor, barrin' this yere chain, to buy land, and you own every inch of it, you say to me, says you, 'You're on my land,' says you. 'Well,' says I, 'I ain't doin' no harm standing here, am I?' 'You're trespassin' ' says you, 'trespassin' on my property, see?' Well, what kin a fellow do? Dead or alive, I got to trespass. No place for me as don't own no land as ain't a trespass to stand or lie down on." 'Well,' says you, 'you let me have a link of that there chain, and I'll let you stand there,' says you."

"But Sam," said I, "your hand has not forgotten its cunning. Can't you make another chain?"

"No, siree!" said Sam emphatically. "Ain't no difference how many chains the under dog makes, land goin' up all the time in price, see? And every chain-maker as

"SO MY CHAIN'S MAKIN' ME A SLAVE, SEE?"

comes over here makes my chain wuth less compared with what I got to pay for standing-room. So my chain's makin' me a slave, see? Soon you'll tell me thet my time is up and thet I am in your way; thet there's another fellow expected here from Europe, and he'll want to stand in my place; and again I dicker for the right by giving you more of my chain, till at last I ain't got none left. Do you call me a *freeman?* I tell you, I am a slave that must needs beg for work, and take what work is thrown to him. Yes, and I, a man who never uses liquor, must sell it to these poor, underpaid, overworked men around here, because I have a wife and children, and dare not give up this situation. Call you this freedom? The South was full of just such freedom before I enlisted and fought through the war to free the black slaves, and never tumbled to the fact that my own arms and legs were soon to have shackles made for 'em. I am a bar-keeper in a one-horse, brown-sugar tavern, and you a millionaire. Can you tell me why?"

Sam rose, and held out his hand, and said, "I did not mean to let drive like that: I only wished to explain why those duffers downstairs won't be friendly and open wid you. It is because they are afraid of you. You might as well see things as they really are. Good-night." And he disappeared in the gloom of the hallway, leaving me alone with my troublesome thoughts.

That there was a something between me and the men, I felt to be true. I could not talk to them without feeling that it was only politeness that made them answer me, for it was evident that I had not their confidence. It was also evident that the dismal weather had affected Sam as well as myself, for in my occasional visits to this place, I had heretofore found him one of the jolliest of fellows, always with a witty remark ready to slip off the end of his tongue or a comical story to relate.

What did he mean by "seeing things as they really are"?

It has been my custom through life not to think of disagreeable things—a custom I have cultivated to such an extent that I have been able, under the most trying circumstances, forcibly to turn my thoughts into pleasant channels. When a friend used me badly, I would not allow my thought to dwell upon it. If the stocks I held went down, I congratulated myself upon possessing other securities that were booming. If, as it once happened off Buzzard's Bay, my foresail was carried away, I opened a bottle, and drank to the health of the mainsail.

So now, following my usual custom, I took my mental self in hand, and com-

SEEING THINGS AS THEY REALLY ARE.—
"WHY, LORD BLESS YOU, SONNY, I'VE NOTHING IN MY BAG FOR YOU!"

menced to plan a yachting cruise for next year. I would have a most charming party, of both sexes, aboard. Delightful I knew it would be, for me at least, for among the guests would be one whose presence never yet had failed to so affect all my surroundings as to make all objects appear beautiful, all sounds seem harmony, all conversation poetry. And as I thought of this, Sam's parting remark, "You might as well see things as they really are," came to my mind unbidden, and so suddenly that I started, thinking for the instant that I had just heard the sentence repeated.

Might it not be possible that, if we did see things as they really are, all would be beautiful? Nature is a divine handiwork, and must be beautiful; and if we saw her in her real light, and compared our impressions, the result must be poetry, and then, possibly, all sound, to our better-educated ears, would make a symphony. The dog whose sense of smell is so remarkably acute that he can follow his master's footsteps over a path trodden by numbers of people, hours after his master has passed; to whom each separate stone, stick, leaf, and bit of vegetation has a separate smell, and who, if he could talk, might say, "A hare passed here," "A partridge sat there," "A child passed this way followed by a lamb," "On this stump sat a cat an hour since"—an animal with such a refined sense of smell as this will sneeze and show every sign of pain and disgust when a perfumed handkerchief is put to its nose, and yet will roll with delight on carrion, for no other purpose than to scent its body with an odor unbearable to its master's duller and comparatively crude sense of smell. The dog undoubtedly has a more highly developed sense of smell than we have, and why is he not a better judge of odors?

I laughed as I thought how pleasant some sections of New York would be if I could only smell things as they really are; and, becoming mentally facetious, I imagined the heaven a man with the dog's keen sense of smell would find on this earth; the sight of an artist, who can see beauty in a discolored door, a battered brass kettle, or a yellow pumpkin; and the ears of a poet, to whom the harsh language with which the plowman addressed his horses or oxen, the roar of a wild beast, the silly talk of an awkward, freckled country girl, appear, when filtered through his cultured ear, as the most perfect harmony;—and, I might add, the happy mental composition of a Fourth of July orator, who sees nothing but what is great and grand in his country.

A Fourth of July orator, by the way—I

thought—I have heard them when I was a lad, but not lately. What jolly times we used to have in the grove, listening to the reading of the Declaration of Independence! And all the country people would bring their lunch with them, and munch it as they listened to the annually repeated words:

> We hold these truths to be self-evident : that all men are created equal; that they are endowed by their Creator with certain unalienable rights; that among these are life, liberty, and the pursuit of happiness.

Why do we not hear it read now as it was when I was a child? Are we conscious that we are, by our lives, giving the lie to it? Bosh! I exclaimed, as I again took a firm hold of my rebellious mind, and tried forcibly to steer it away from the rocks I saw ahead. As I did so, I was conscious, for the first time, that I did not wish to see things as they really are, for fear the truth might be unpleasant to me; yet, while I was conscious of this, I did not admit it to myself, but, losing my grip for a time, I allowed my annoyance to manifest itself in mental railings against society, politics, church and state—in fact, against everything except myself.

At last, jumping up from my seat, I paced

the floor, exclaiming, "What ails me anyhow? What ails Sam? And what did he mean by his parting shot, 'You might as well see things as they really are'?" "I wish I could!" I exclaimed impatiently. "I wish I could!" I repeated thoughtfully. "I wish I could only see things as they really are, and not as a diseased imagination makes them appear," I said at last earnestly; and as I again seated myself, the words were repeated mentally. The pattering rain outside took up the strain, and repeated over and over again, with the tireless monotony of machinery—I wish I could see things as they really are, I wish I could see things as they really are, I wish, etc.

CHAPTER II.

THE bedroom was just as I had left it—the vellum book on the floor, and the light burning. I picked up the book, and without daring to look at the gaudy initials, replaced it carefully upon the bookshelf, and took down another volume bound in red pigskin. On the back, in gold paint, was the simple word, "Magus"; below that the bearded figure of a man, with long finger and toe nails. The figure had on his head a high-topped, royal crown, and held an arrow in his right hand, the point of which rested over the eye of a dragon, between whose batlike wings this strange personage sat, with his legs hanging on both sides. At the bottom was the legend, "Bene Lightmans, London, 1601."

Ah! Here I had something that I knew could only amuse me—a real old book of magic, a book of old superstitions. Although witchcraft is supposed to be a thing of the past among enlightened people, yet who can deny that much of the superstition upon which it was built still lurks in the most enlightened minds?—that is, if you count yourselves among the enlightened ones.

Whether this is imbibed with our mother's milk, or grafted upon the tender mind of childhood by superstitious old nurses, it matters not: we have every day indisputable evidence that it is there, and I suppose I have my share; and, possibly, the leaven of superstition in my mental composition helped to lend a charm to this old pigskin-covered book, with its bedeviled back and strangely figured leaves.

Once again my interest as a bookworm was aroused; once again I lighted my pipe, and, comfortably fixed in my chair before the stove, I resolved to make a night of it— not with the poor, degraded, hunted-looking wretches that frequented the bar, but with the fantastical whims and nonsense of our ancestors—nonsense for which many a poor old woman and many a good man paid dearly in the old days, when fagots and bonfires were used as expressions of faith in the power of cabalistic signs. Thank God, those days are over, and a man may now

read unmolested whatsoever pleases his fancy!

The publisher of the book I now held in my hands, solemnly and apparently in good faith opens with a definition of witchcraft, especially in women, and goes on to state, in his own peculiar style, as follows:

PUBLISHER'S PREFACE. [TRANSLATED FROM THE ORIGINAL LATIN.]

WE have infinite instances of witchcraft in history which it were not fair to set aside merely because they are not reconcilable to our personal philosophy; but, as it happens, there is something in real philosophy to countenance them.

All living things, we know, emit effluvia, both by the breath and the pores of the skin. All bodies, therefore, within the sphere of their perspiratory or expiratory effluvia will be affected by them; and that, in this or another manner, according to the quality of the effluvia; and in this or that degree, according to the disposition of the emittent and the recipient parts. In confirmation thereof, we need only call attention to infectious diseases conveyed by effluvia.

Now, of all parts of an animal body, the eye, we know, is the quickest. It moves with the greatest celerity and in all variety of directions. Again, its coats and humours are as permeable as any other part of the body (witness the rays of light it so copiously receives). The eye, therefore, no doubt, emits its effluvia like the other parts. The fine humours of the eye must be continually exhaling. The heat of the pervading rays will rarefy and attenuate them; and that, with the subtile juice or spirit of the neighboring optic nerve, supplied in great abundance by the vicinity of the brain, must make a fund of volatile matter to be dispensed, and, as it were, determined by the eye. For, as Tacitus remarks on the savage figures of the Germans, the eyes of men are first overcome in battle.

Here, then, we have both the dart and the hand to fling it—the one furnished with all the force and vehemence, and the other with all the sharpness and activity, one would require. No wonder if their effects be great.

Do but conceive the eye as a sling, capable of the swiftest and intensest motions and vibrations; and, again, as communicating with a source of such matter as the nervous juice elaborated in the brain—a matter so subtile and penetrating that it is supposed to fly instantaneously through the solid capillaments of the nerves; and so active and forcible that it distends and convulses the muscles and distorts the limbs and alters the whole habitude of the body, giving motion and action to a mass of inert, inactive matter. A projectile of such a nature, flung by such an engine as the eye, must have an effect wherever it strikes.

This theory, we are of the opinion, fully accounts for that branch of witchcraft called fascination. That man is not secure from fascination is matter of easy observation. Few people but have, again and again, felt the effects of an angry, a fierce, a commanding, a disdainful, a lascivious, an entreating eye, etc. These effects, no doubt, are owing to the different ejaculations of the eye, and are a degree of witchcraft.

Following this description, and serving as a sort of tail-piece, is a colored illustration of an eye, encircled by words in strange characters. It is, or at least it appeared to me then, an uncanny object. But this explanation of the power of witchcraft entertained me, and struck me as being ingenious, and I was amused and interested when the publisher promised that the author would teach the reader how to do many wonderful things, until, like the dwarf in "Valentine and Orson," "he would learn so much of the arte of nygromancy that, above all others, he would be perfyte;" but what particularly interested me was the promise that the art of the transmutation of metals would also be taught. I turned to the page indicated as containing this secret (for which I have no apology to offer, and can only say that if my reader would have preferred the part which told of the wonderful bone from the right side of Pliny's red toad,

"I WISH I COULD SEE THINGS AS THEY REALLY ARE."

which, if removed and placed in water, would cause the water to boil, and, if administered in food to a lady, would cause a degree of love for the donor equal in intensity to boiling water, the reader is welcome to his choice). What I wanted to know was how to turn the baser metals into gold. With that secret I would form a syndicate of one person that would make the Standard Oil, sugar trust, and railroads turn green with envy; and I could then hunt for the red toad of Pliny if I wished. However, having already gained the affections of, to my mind, the most beautiful and loveliest girl in Pennsylvania, Pliny and his red toad possessed no great attractions for me.

Now, all this time, while my thoughts, reacting from their former gloomy turn, were wandering among the mysteries of the book of magic in a jolly, reckless, yet, although unconsciously, a half-serious manner, I was involuntarily repeating to myself, "I wish I could see things as they really are," so that it seemed as if I had a dual mind, one of which was occupied with the sentence just quoted, and the other with the old book before me.

Again I was doomed to disappointment, for, as I read, in place of the nonsense I expected, this was what met my eye:

Beware of flattery, self-love, and covetousness, so wilt thou thrive; and be diligent in thy occupation, so shall thy body be fed. Idleness is offensive to the Deity. Industry shall sweeten thy brown bread, and the fruits of it shall warm thy heart with gratitude to Him that blesses thee with *enough*. Seek for no more, for it will *damn thee*. It has been said by Him who never spoke in vain, *that man shall get bread by the sweat of his brow*.

I hurriedly turned over the leaves, for I

was not looking for moral lessons, especially in the devil's book. At last I found the directions I was in search of.

"I wish I could see things as they really are," said one member of my dual mind. "And I believe I am beginning to," replied the other. "Can it not be possible that beneath all this apparent nonsense some great truths are hidden? What are all these circles and signs? Where did they come from? Directly handed down from the Magi of the East—symbols of a masonry that antedates masonry, and is, perhaps, the father of masonry."

I once again turned to my book, and read:

> When thy spiritual eye is opened, thou shalt begin to see to what end thou wert created, thou shalt want no necessary thing, either for thy comfort or support. Only keep the rules: Love thy neighbor as thyself; arrogate nothing to thine own power, for he who desires spiritual knowledge cannot obtain it by any means but by first purifying his own heart.

These are strange words for a humbug, a common necromancer, a fake! Might it not be possible that, in the dark ages of persecution and violence, when wise men were wont to hold their tongues between their teeth, to escape the alternative of having them dragged from their mouths, they had recourse to cipher, understood only by the initiated? We all know that some people claim that by a system or science of correspondences they can explain most beautifully many mysterious chapters of Holy Writ. I began to wonder whether the old alchemists, who claimed to be able to manufacture gold, might not have told the truth, not in the sense I had always supposed they meant, but in a higher and better sense.

"I wish I could see things as they really are," continued to repeat the pattering rain; and again before my mind rose the image of the chain-gang of slaves; but this time I felt no alarm, and gradually I saw that it was the string of miners, with begrimed faces, that I had confused with the picture of negroes; at the same time I was aware of the fact that the clanking dinner-pails might indeed represent the chains of the negroes. Was not I a part owner of that slave-gang of American citizens? The thought went through me like an electric shock.

Again I turned to the strange volume, and read:

When thou shalt have so far purified thy heart, as we

have spoken is indispensably necessary for the receiving every good thing, thou shalt then see with other eyes than thou dost at present. Thy spiritual eye will be opened, and thou shalt read man as plain as thou wilt our books. . . . All philosophers agree that, the first matter being found, we may proceed without much difficulty, for the *Prima Materia*, I say, is to be found in ourselves; we all possess the *Prima Materia*, from the beggar to the king. . . . I pray thee, my friend, look into thyself, and endeavor to find out in what part of thy composition is this *Prima Materia* of the *lapis philosophorum*, or of what part of thy substance can the first matter be drawn out.

"In myself, then, is this *Prima Materia*," said I, closing the book, "and in myself must I look for it if I wish to see things as they really are, and read men as books. The crude metal—the lead, the mercury, the iron—is the slave-gangs, with their begrimed faces, and of them I can make so much pure gold."

I opened the volume again, and my gaze was riveted upon the strange, colored drawing of the eye; and as I stared at it, wondering at the peculiar fascination it seemed now to exert over me, my dual mind kept up its refrain of, "I wish I could see things as they really are."

Suddenly a peculiar and indescribable sensation took possession of my nerves. My chest seemed broader and deeper, my arms stronger, my frame larger; but I dreaded to look toward the mirror, and in avoiding it I noticed that bands of light, like electric light in color, were streaming past the edges of the window-blind into my room, making the lamplight look a bright orange by contrast. I pulled up the blind. It was dawn. The clouds were rolling up the mountain like great rolls of raw cotton, and the light-blue sky shone, clear and beautiful, in the spaces between the fleeing vapor. " A nor'west wind, cool and clear."

As the curtains of mist were lifted, I could see for miles through the transparent air; and as the sunlight burst forth, each drop of rain that lingered on twig or branch became a miniature sun that reflected back the glitter of its great king in the sky. A belated robin, that seemed somewhat confused in regard to his calendar, commenced a wild, hilarious "Chee-wink, chee-wee," evidently under the impression that his winter migration was over, and spring had come again.

Again a file of miners passed, trudging through the mud. The merry song of the bird had no effect upon them, and I saw them as they really were—a band of degraded, disheartened slaves. I read them as I might a book, and in this human book I read my own disgrace. I, an American, whose father fought to free the black slaves of the South, whose grandfather fought in the war of 1812 to free the sea of slave sailors, whose great-grandfather fought for that grand document which declared that all men were born free and equal—I, the American, in the "land of the free and the home of the brave," was part owner of a band of miserable white slaves, and was here, in this town, in this little hotel, the American House—for what purpose? Principally to consult with the other slave-drivers about restricting the output of coal, that I and they might raise its price by causing untold suffering to these already miserable miners, and add to the expense of living for the poor, taxed, and rack-rented people of the city—that we might have more money to spend on yachts!

I almost wished that the cursed pigskin-covered book, with its companion in vellum, had been destroyed before I could have read them, moonling that I was. Moonblight? It was only temporary. I now *knew* that I was sane, but untold wealth could not tempt me to look into the glass.

It was a custom of mine to shave myself

each morning, and I wore neither beard nor mustache. My razor was acknowledged by all my boon companions on board the yacht to be the best, and there had always been much wise talk about this and that soap, razor, and strop, as we tested the keen edges of our favorite blades each morning after our plunge in the Sound or in the harbor. But of what use was a beautiful razor, with no glass to shave by? I made one attempt to do without a glass, but the blood flowed so copiously

"THE CURSED PIGSKIN-COVERED BOOK."

that it was some time before I could make a piece of court-plaster adhere to my chin. I then carefully wiped the razor dry, replaced it in its case, and proceeded with my toilet. I put on clean linen, but when it came to tying my four-in-hand scarf, I was in a fix. I had never tried it before without a glass ; but after a while I made a knot that felt all right, and stuck my scarf-pin in. The remainder was plain sailing. My shoes were muddy from the day before, and I started down stairs to get a little hump-backed hanger-on of the hotel to black them for me. This hump-backed man, or boy, was a favorite of mine ; he was always so polite and withal so witty and bright that I generally paid him with a silver quarter in place of the customary five-cent nickel,—five cents for the shine and twenty because he amused me. I found "Humpy,' as he was called, sweeping out the office or bar-room ; his back was toward me. When he heard my voice, he turned with a pleasant good-morning.

Great Goodness! Was that the man to whom I had been tossing money, as one would to an amusing negro in slavery times? Could it be possible that I was ass enough

to treat him as an inferior being—a dog, who, when he sits up on his hind legs and begs, is to be rewarded with a lump of sugar? I blushed, stammered, but, for the life of me, could not frame the words. I was ashamed to ask him to black my boots. Why? Because I read him as a book—I saw him as he really was. There was no hump on the real man's back, there was nothing comic in the real man's expression; but there was a grandeur I had never seen before, a nobility I had often pictured, but seldom seen. It seemed almost as if his face shone; and when he smiled, and asked me if I wanted a shine this morning, it appeared as if some one else was speaking. I could not make the words fit the person I saw. I was about to decline, when, as if anticipating me, he said, "I'm glad that you're here, boss, 'cause I need that quarter dis morning, you bet!" Mechanically I seated myself; but when he bent his little humped back, and brought his face over my shoe, I could not sit there. So, quickly handing him his fee, I said, "What's your name?" "Humpy," he replied. "No; your real name?" "Nathaniel James." "Well, Nate," said I, "if you will kindly excuse me, I won't take a shine this morning. I don't like to sit still. I didn't sleep well last night, and am nervous."

He looked up at me with eyes that, I was conscious, read me through. He also saw men with his spiritual eyes, and I felt more embarrassed than before, when I knew this to be true.

Never before do I remember feeling ashamed to meet a fellow-man's eye. I had always prided myself on being perfectly square in my dealings with all men, and, having nothing to be ashamed of, I felt no dread of any one; but now the case was changed. Here was a man whose character, aims, and life were so far above mine that I dare not expose myself to his glance; so, hastily turning my back, I started for the barber-shop; but with the door-knob in my hand I stopped short. There were mirrors in front of each chair, so that the customers might survey themselves during all stages of the treatment by the tonsorial artists in charge. If there was one person on earth that I did not want to see as he really was, that person was myself. So I went to the breakfast-room with my shoes unblacked and my face unshaven—acts of which I had not been guilty within ten years at least. However, there was fortunately no one at my end of the table; and I took up the small, damp piece of cloth which served as a napkin, and, taking care to look at no one, I ate my breakfast as it was served.

CHAPTER III.

THE people of the town had all noticed a change in me, and from the significant looks, nods, and winks, I readily understood that they one and all considered that I was slightly demented, or, as Sam expressed it, "They think ye'r a little off." But I knew better. My mind had never been healthier, clearer, and brighter, nor my perceptions keener; and, while I was conscious of the fact that the new powers I possessed were very imperfect, yet the change was wonderful to me.

My physical health also was most robust. Each morning, when I rose, it was with no touch of languor, but with an exhilarated feeling, as if I had just had a shower and a rub down after a brisk row in a single shell. I drank no spirituous liquor, because, being in a natural state of mind and body, I needed no drug to produce an artificial sensation of health and spirits; in fact, any preparation of alcohol appeared to me as abhorrent as castor-oil, quinine, or any other concoction

"I HAD ATTENDED A MEETING OF MINE OWNERS."

made by physicians for weak and sick humanity.

I had attended a meeting of mine owners. I saw before me a crowd of men, most of whom I knew; that is, I had always supposed that I knew them—a well-dressed, polite party of men. But I could see below the surface. Each one seemed to think that his neighbor was glass, and he himself opaque, while to me all were so transparent that it appeared as if I were in an assemblage of children.

Mr. Keene, whom we always looked up to as a regular Napoleon in business, I was disappointed in. It appeared manifest that his whole success came from keeping his countenance placid, with a knowing look in his eye, while his mind was barren absolutely, without a plan or an original thought; yet he was a smart man for all that, and his smartness consisted in simply waiting until some one else suggested a bright idea, and then, with the knowing look and placid face, immediately appropriating the idea. Rising to his feet, he would state, in a very patronizing manner, that the only practical suggestion so far had come from Mr. Brown, and it coincided with his preconceived plans exactly. Thereupon he would paraphrase Mr. Brown's suggestion in such a manner that Mr. Brown would feel highly complimented, while Mr. Keene would wear the laurels that properly belonged to Mr. Brown. I saw this repeated over and over again, yet no one else seemed to be aware of it.

No one paid any attention to me except by a good-natured smile or nod. They evidently thought, with the villagers, that I was a "little off." My beard by this time was stubby and my mustache of about the consistency of a worn-out tooth-brush. My hair needed trimming, but my linen was neat, and I had learned to black my own shoes, and paid "Humpy" his quarter a day for some less menial service.

At this meeting I listened until they had about decided upon a plan of action which I saw at once was bound to work great hardship among the miners and the poor consumers in the city. Then I rose and pointed out these facts to them.

"Business is business," said Mr. Keene. "Our business is to look out for *our* interests; that of others to look out for *theirs*. I think that settles it."

Now it so happened that the arrangement about to be agreed upon would benefit Mr. Keene more than any present, and would even be a great disadvantage to two others present. This I saw in Mr. Keene's mind; although he was not bright enough to suggest the proposed plan, he could see how advantageous it would be to him; for as he saw it, I read his thoughts and saw it too. So, when they tried to shut me off with cries of "Question! Question!" I simply stood there until there was a lull, and then said:

"Mr. Chairman, I believe I have the floor?"

"You have, sir, unless you wish to resign it to facilitate business."

"I will do so in a few moments," I replied.

A tired look crept over each face, as the members of the conference settled back in their chairs, not to listen, but to endure.

"Gentlemen," I said, "you really must not go into this thing blindly. Next to Mr. Keene himself, I would be the one most benefited financially by this arrangement; but there is Mr. Brown, who suggested the idea, and Mr. White, who approved of it: they will be absolute losers if they keep to their agreement."

Mr. Brown and Mr. White looked interested. Mr. Keene jumped to his feet, and wanted to know if I had not just stated that Mr. Brown himself suggested the idea. Not noticing the interruption, I proceeded to put into words all that I saw in Mr. Keene's mind, and a hubbub followed. Cries of "Question!" "Order!" "Move we adjourn!" "Previous question!" were heard on all sides. Mr. White, a greedy, vindictive, and heartless fellow, with the polish of a courtier and the mind of a savage, owing

Mr. Keene a grudge for some past transaction, was loud in his denunciation of this gentleman, who, he claimed, was using the conference to further his own individual interest; and, to my astonishment, this savage pointed out how Mr. Keene was willing to commit any injustice to the poor, toiling miners, even to drive them past the verge of starvation, if by that means he could make a dollar or two; and the pathetic picture he drew of the effect upon the poor laborer brought tears to the eyes of many present. But the chairman hammered with his gavel, and ruled Mr. White out of order.

Now, amid all this, I saw that these men, who were coolly planning to rob the people of so much money, were not naturally bad men. Most of them were what are considered charitable people.

After I sat down, I received no more smiles and good-natured nods. Mr. Keene looked at me with that placid face and knowing look, as if he would say, "You're a sharp one. I see through your move!" But I knew that he did not, because my move was too simple; there was nothing behind what I had said, and I could not help smiling to see Keene's troubled mind taking one view and then another, trying to see in what way I was to be benefited financially by opposing his motion.

The thought that I was acting in a disinterested manner never entered a mind present. As I turned from face to face, I could see that all except Mr. Brown and Mr. White were puzzling themselves just as Mr. Keene was. Mr. Brown and Mr. White were concocting schemes to put Keene in a hole, as they would have termed it, and they looked upon me as their ally, never taking time to question my motives, satisfied with the fact that, for some reason of my own, I would help them. But no one of them all thought that I was not perfectly sound mentally, although I could see that Mr. Keene and some others intended to treat me as an irresponsible party the next time I was in their way.

I have related how the assembly appeared to me as an assembly. As individuals the phenomenon was strange indeed; when some casual or accidental remark appealed to the true man in any one of them, I could see him (the true man, I mean), always handsome, always strong, always bright; but as the lower impulses were in turn made prominent, while the clothes, the hair, or the features were not altered, an expression would steal over his face that was sometimes ludicrous (or at least so it appeared to me before I fully appreciated its meaning), sometimes disgusting and revolting, and sometimes terrible, but never pleasant.

Mr. Keene, for instance, would so resemble a fox at times, that I could scarcely believe him human; and yet there were the

"A RED-MOUTHED WOLF WITH WHITE FANGS."

same nose, eyes, mouth and brow that I had always known, and thought strikingly handsome, and even while I was studying him to detect just what it was that made him look like a fox, I realized that there was no fox there, but a red-mouthed wolf, with white fangs showing, ready to rend and devour any of the pack that was unfortunate enough to be crippled or killed; and, even in the midst of this appearance, I could plainly see the well-known features that I had so long admired for their manly beauty. Once or twice only did I see a trace of the real man in him, and that was so transient that I could scarce make up my mind it really existed.

Mr. White, in spite of his fashionable and expensive dress, his closely shaven face, his immaculate linen, and his trained smile, did not deceive me; for, while I could see these with my natural eyes, and know that they existed, I could also see the true expression of the inner Mr. White, and it was that of a rattlesnake. The rapid manner in which he addressed the chairman before launching into his remarks constantly reminded me of

"I COULD ALSO SEE THE TRUE EXPRESSION OF THE INNER MR. WHITE."

the vicious, dry, singing noise made by a rattlesnake before striking; but when he drew the pathetic picture of the poor starved slaves of the coal-pit, the snake expression had left him, and something in his appearance brought to my mind one of those spiders hidden in a rose, whose swollen body and thin legs, partaking of the color of the flower, look so like the harmless plant that they are unnoticed by the busy bumblebee until, just as the latter thinks he has secured the treasures of the rose, he feels the poisonous fangs of the enemy in his head, and, benumbed by the poison, dies with hardly a struggle.

Ofttimes these transformations seemed only thoughts flitting through my mind; then again they appeared so real that it was with difficulty that I retained sufficient control of my feelings to prevent showing my abhorrence or terror by exclamations or precipitate retreat. Such action on my part would, I knew, confirm the suspicions of my mental derangement and put an end to any chance I might have of being useful to my fellow-men in helping them to avoid the pitfalls I now began to see plainly.

During the meeting, and always while the

financial interests were under discussion, the real man seldom showed himself in any of the assembly ; but he more frequently shone through and ennobled the countenance during the conversation upon subjects that did not touch the pocket.

Once, when a question of agreeing upon the form of a lease that would evade the eviction laws for the protection of the miners was broached, I became so disgusted that it was with the greatest effort I could restrain some exclamation ; for, before me I saw, not an assemblage of gentlemen, but a lot of parasitic insects, covering the body of the miner, and sucking his blood. It was only an instant that the impression lasted, yet it was extremely vivid while it remained, and the strangest part of it was that, at the time, I saw no reason for such an appearance, but I knew that there must be one.

I was so much interested in what I saw that each day appeared all too short. Ten days had passed. The meeting of mine owners, thanks to my remarks, broke up without coming to any decision. My business was all finished, yet still I lingered in the gloomy, straggling town.

Not many miles away lived the lady of

my choice, the girl whose gentle heart, refined and educated mind, shone through a face as charming as any to be found. She was waiting for me anxiously, and each day I received a letter from her in which she expressed great concern for my health. There was nothing to detain me, and I had been counting for months upon this opportunity of visiting her at her home; still I postponed my visit.

This may seem strange, but, since I am making a clean breast of my experiences, I may as well own up to the fact that I dreaded her as much as I did my mirror. Not that I could see myself reflected in her sweet eyes in any but a complimentary manner, but—ashamed as I am now, and was then, of the fear—I was afraid to see even her as she really was.

I was rich; she had but little. I was esteemed a "good catch"; she was admired for her acknowledged beauty; and many a fellow, in my hearing, had deplored the fact that she had not a fortune. That was before I met her; since then, they only congratulated me on my luck in securing such a prize.

I could recall several instances where friends of mine had become engaged to ladies who, to them, possessed all the virtues and beauties of the sex combined, but to me, were foolish, simpering girls, or cold, selfish, affected creatures. I wondered what my friends could see in them that was attractive, much less, lovable; and yet I knew that they loved these girls with a true devotion, and were men of good taste. If these fellows were blinded by Cupid, why not I? If I was blinded, it was such a heavenly blindness that I dreaded the restoration of my eyesight, and feared as much to see my darling as she appeared to others, and might really be, as I did to see my own cowardly face in the glass.

And so, day by day I postponed my visit, and spent the time inspecting my mines.

CHAPTER IV.

PROF. FOLLIUM is an old friend of mine, a naturalist and a geologist, and a man whose general knowledge is extensive. I had had many a delightful talk with him upon books and nature, and never left him without a pleasant impression and a feeling that I had gained some knowledge by his discourse. Naturally, in my present state, he came to my mind, and I wondered that I had not thought of him before, knowing that he was in town, collecting specimens from the mines to add to his already large collection, and to illustrate his lectures.

I started off immediately in search of the professor, and found him, hammer in hand, just starting upon an expedition.

"Good morning, Professor," I said.

"Good morning," he replied. "I've been

expecting to see you. Heard you were in town. Heard you raised a rumpus at the meeting, the other day. I congratulate you, my boy! I knew there was good stuff in you!" And the professor smiled over the rims of his glasses as he extended his hand cordially and grasped mine.

"Professor, I come for advice. I am in trouble. I see wrong all around me, and appear helpless to prevent it. What is the cause of all this?"

The professor looked sober a moment, and shook his head as he replied, "It is man. God never creates a wrong."

"Do you mean," I said, "that it is our constant evasion or breaking of the law that is at fault?"

"Law?" said the professor. "Law, my boy, is never at fault. In the nature of things, it is impossible." Again he shook his head, paused a moment, and repeated, "Law? Law is perfect."

I smiled, and was about to make some facetious remark, when the professor reverently removed his hat, gazed around at the mountains and landscape for a moment, then solemnly repeated, as if to himself, "Law? I acknowledge but one law, and that is the

law that I see ruling the universe, everywhere present and everywhere active, and never broken. If I attempt to break that part of it called gravitation, and step from the roof of a tall house, my mangled remains will testify that the law is unbroken." Then turning and addressing his remarks to me he continued: "Talk about martyrs to religion, to principle, to honesty! Personally, I never saw one; but martyrs to crime, to filth, to greed, I see everywhere. Go to our prisons, go to our hospitals, our insane-asylums. All are filled with martyrs to crime, suffering the torments of hell for the sake—and only for the sake—of trying to break the plain laws of nature.

"When a botanist wishes an Alpine plant, he climbs the mountain; and there, 'mid the glaciers, or in the track of the avalanche, he finds the object of his search, because the atmosphere and the surroundings produce the conditions necessary for the existence of the plant. When he wishes an aquatic plant, he seeks the valley, and in the lakes, rivers or marshes finds the object of his search, because the atmosphere and the surroundings produce it. When a naturalist wishes to procure a certain kind of animal, he seeks that spot where the atmosphere and the surroundings produce just the conditions necessary for that animal, and there he finds the object of his search. A sportsman would never go to the plains and the valleys in search of big-horn or chamois, but amidst the cloud-capped mountains; because there the atmos-

IF MIGHT IS RIGHT, THIS IS A TYPE OF THE MODERN SO-CALLED CHRISTIAN.

phere and the surroundings produce the conditions necessary for these animals' existence. A detective would never go to the homes of the workingmen in search of a defaulting bank president; but to Wall Street, the faro-table, the race-course, or some place where people acquire money without work, because there the atmosphere and the surroundings produce and suit defaulters.

"Show me a government founded and conducted on the principles of justice and equal rights to all men, and I will show you the highest type of manhood, intelligence, industry and prosperity, because the atmosphere and surroundings produce it. Show me a tyrannical and unjust government, and I will show you vice, squalor, poverty and crime, because the atmosphere and surroundings produce them. Now if, in our own country, we see waiters cringing and bowing for a tip; railroad employees and baggage-men putting their manhood in their pockets for the sake of the quarter that goes with it; miners living like starved vermin in the blackened and begrimed shanties of Pennsylvania; gentlemen, so-called, living lives of debauchery; people starving in the streets of the cities; tramps, anarchists and Pinkerton bullies—it is because the atmosphere and the surroundings produce them. My dear fellow," said the genial professor, again resuming his pleasant smile, "we are ourselves to blame for all the misery we see around us. I confess that my studies have not been directed in this line, but I know, from my knowledge of Nature, that she makes no mistakes. There is an ample feast provided by her for man, and this country has riches untold and incalculable, which need only labor to bring them forth; and yet, owing to the greed of a few of us, and the thoughtlessness of many, we keep those treasures locked up, while our fellow-men die by the wayside for want of the necessaries of life. I see that you know this much yourself. Then do as I do with all my problems—commence at the beginning. Commence with a babe. A baby is born. It has eyes: that means that it was intended to see. It has ears: that means that it was intended to hear. It has a mouth to receive nourishment: that means that nourishment is provided for it. It has neither wings nor fins, but feet: that means that it must walk, and is a land animal, and must have land to walk on. All these things will teach you that it has an inherent right to light, air, water and food; to procure the latter it has hands to transform the products of the earth into a suitable form by labor. I have already said that Nature has provided untold wealth for the babe, yet we will not allow it to use its hands, unless it does so for us. Now, then, it seems to me that we—meaning you and me, and the rest of humanity—are the ones to blame if this or any babe dies from want and starvation ; and the cause lies in us, not in the law."

"Yes," I replied; "the *prima materia* is in ourselves, and there we must look for it if we expect to turn the cruder metals into pure gold."

"Oh ho!" exclaimed the little man, as he took off his spectacles to look at me the better. "So, so! You've been trying to find the solution in the black-book, eh?"

"Well, a well-balanced mind can find food in almost any book; and I must say it always appeared to me that there must be some hidden treasures locked up in those old books of so-called magic."

"It is not many years ago that all chemists and physicians were considered magicians. But don't let yourself be led astray by wild fancies. Apply this test to everything—can it be demonstrated? If so, adopt it without fear, for it is the truth, and truth is divine. If an Indian or Chinaman makes a statement, do not disparage it. If it can be demonstrated, it is true; if not, it is false. If I and other college professors make a statement, tell us to demonstrate it. If it can be demonstrated, it is true; if not, it is false. Believe nothing that is incapable of demonstration, except the fact that you exist, and are a living soul. Apply this test, and sooner or later, you will find out the cause of the terrible wrong, the dire want, the squalor, the crime, the abrutement of our brothers, keeping their place alongside of a hotbed growth of civilization of the most brilliant type. And now, lad, I must be off. This is more of a lecture on political economy than I ever remember delivering before. Only one word more. If you are going into this thing in earnest (and I believe you are), when you find the cause let me know; and if you can demonstrate it, as I require my pupils to do, with a piece of chalk on the blackboard, you may count me as a convert. Good-bye!" And gathering up his bag and hammer the man of science departed.

After bidding good-bye to the professor, I went directly to the hotel-bar to look for Sam, and found him practising at twirling a spoon in a glass of water, though the expert manner in which he did it seemed to require no practice to render it perfect.

"Good morning, Sam," was my greeting.

"Good morning, sir," he replied, without taking his eyes from the glass, or ceasing to make the little spoon spin around in a most marvelous manner.

"What are you up to, Sam?" I asked.

"Oh, nothing, sir; just practising making a cocktail."

There were no customers in, only two or three gray-haired old men sitting in the heavy wooden-armed chairs peculiar to country bar-rooms; and these old fellows were dreaming the day away, or reading, with their eyes only, the daily papers. Their old eyes were none too good, for the frosty-headed men held the papers close against their noses as they read; but they were all too absorbed in vacancy to heed me, so I plunged right in to what was uppermost in my mind.

"Sam," I said, "are you an anarchist?"

"No, sir," he replied gravely.

"Are you a socialist?"

"No, sir," he again answered, "unless Abe Lincoln and Thomas Jefferson were socialists; and from what I have read in socialistic speeches I don't think they were."

"What are you, Sam?"

"I, sir?" Sam dropped the spoon, and

straightened himself up to his full height. "I, sir," he repeated, "I am an *American!*"

"Well, I know that much from what you have already told me."

"You don't catch on," said Sam, with a face that ill accorded with his slangy speech. "I am an American in principle. I believe

PREJUDICE.

in chucking the tea overboard, widout taking the trouble to work the Injun racket either. I believe in the inspired"—Sam said "inspired" in a hesitating manner, as if he was not quite sure that it was proper form to use so high-sounding a word, but gaining courage from my looks, he continued—"I believe in the inspired document called the Declaration of Independence. I believe, with Abe Lincoln and Thomas Jefferson, that there should be *no involuntary servitude except for crime.*"

" So do I, Sam, so do I. But what of that ? "

" What of thet ? " said the bar-keeper fiercely, his black eyebrows knitting, as he twirled his heavy moustache until it stood out in two spikes at each side of his face, " what of thet ? Why, thet is as rank treason to-day as old Paddy Henry's talk before der Revolution; and if things go on as they are for a mighty short time longer, der duffer who says thet will be called an anarchist and an agitator. If I could run a talking-mill, like some fellers I know, and could fire off dictionary lingo off-hand, I'd stump der United States on my own hook, and give it to 'em straight wherever I could catch a crowd to talk to. Oh, these crawling and sneaking men that steal our votes wid der money they rob us of! These ornery curs thet rob us of our wages, and then dole it out to us in charity! These hypocritical hirelings that desecrate the Sabbath every Sunday by preaching bosh because they 'r too cowardly to tell what the Bible means! I ain't much of a Christian,

but t'other day I thought I'd see if der
Bible had any such bosh in it. I tell yer,
Mister, I was ready to throw up my hat when
I read it, and how these sniveling old sneaks

"NOW, MISTER, WHAT DOES THET MEAN?"

can read thet book and live is past me! Why,
they seem ter think the Great Creator ain't
got no sense at all, and can be fooled as easy
as a voter; and der tricks they try ter fool him
wid are so thin that a lad can see t'rough

'em—building big churches wid der money stole from us, and then a-plastering them all over wid their own monograms, giving conscience-money back to us in der shape of hospitals, asylums, and libraries, and then a-plastering their ornery names all over *them!* And the fust thing I struck in thet grand book was 'Take heed that ye do not your alms before men *to be seen of them.*' Now, mister, what does thet mean? In another place, it told us not to blow a trumpet before giving alms. What does thet mean? I ain't superstitious and don't go much on luck; but I just 'lowed that book to open fer itself, and then would read the fust thing that caught my eye; and whew! how St. Jeems goes for the rich. 'Woe to ye!' he says—oh, he was onter 'em—'Go to now, ye rich men, and weep and howl, for your miseries shall come upon you!' Then he gives them dead away in another verse about the wages they kept back by fraud. Well, sir, I could hardly believe thet was written so long ago, it hit 'em so hard right now."

"Sam, Sam!" I exclaimed, "I am afraid you did not read the book in the right spirit. There is nothing, as I remember it, vindictive in the New Testament."

"Thet's so," said Sam solemnly, "thet's so. What it says there, ain't for the sake of cussing them, but as a warning, and thet's the way I took it; but I did feel a bit vindictive just now, when I thought of my old landlord a-howlin'. But he, poor cuss, can't help himself any more than I can. You see,

"NOW, MISTER, WHAT DOES THET MEAN?"

Mister, if he lets me have der rent any cheaper than market price he is giving me der diff. in charity. The truth is, there's no such thing as cheap rent. Where it looks cheap, it's 'cause it won't bring any more, thet's all; and I 'spect, if I were a landlord, I'd hev to do the same. Now, ain't it a blamed mean sort of law thet makes a fellow a robber or a robbed man, say?"

"Now, look here, Sam. While I can't help but acknowledge there is something fundamentally wrong, I am hardly prepared to own that I am a robber; but I will own up to even that, if you can demonstrate it to me. Mind now! demonstrate it like a problem on the blackboard, and prove the demonstration."

"Thet's easy, mister, mighty durned easy. What's thet you've got your hand on?"

"My watch-chain," I replied, a little puzzled.

"Where did yer get it?"

All bar-keepers are inclined to be impudent, or, as they themselves would term it, "fresh," if you allow them liberties; but I knew that Sam had some object in view, so I answered, "At the jeweler's."

"Where did he get it?"

"At the manufacturer's."

"Where did the factory get the gold?"

"Well, I suppose you want to know where the gold comes from, eh?"

"Just so. From the mines, from the earth," said Sam.

"You are right."

"WHAT DOES THIS MEAN, MISTER, SAY?"

"Where did yer hat come from? Where did yer clothes come from?"

"Hold on, Sam. My clothes came from sheep."

"Thet's so; but where did the stuff thet made the wool grow come from?"

"The grass? Oh, that grew in the pasture, I suppose."

"Yes; it also came from the earth. Where did yer shoes come from? Earth," he said, answering his own query. "Where did yer stockings come from? Earth," he repeated. "Where does yer food come from? Earth. Now, yer see, the fellow thet owns der earth owns the base of supplies, as we used ter say in der army; and if we could catch on ter der enemy's base of supplies, and hold it, der enemy was ours widout any more fighting, 'cause, soon as they used up what they had, they would starve, unless they came ter us as prisoners of war. Now, then, mister, a few men — a mighty few, too — own the United States and the earth,* the base of

* FROM THOMAS G. SHEARMAN, THE WELL-KNOWN NEW YORK STATISTICIAN.—"The average annual income of the richest hundred Englishmen is about $450,000; but the average annual income of the richest hundred Americans cannot be less than $1,200,000, and probably exceeds $1,500,000. The richest of the Rothschilds, and the world-renowned banker, Baron Overstone, each left about

supplies fer the hull of us. Thet's the reason we are prisoners of war! Thet's the reason we are slaves! Thet's the reason I tend bar! Thet's the reason them fellers live all their lives under ground, piling up money fer you fellers, see?"

Well, I did begin to have a glimmering of light; but I was not ready to give in yet; so I said:

$17,000,000. Earl Dudley, the owner of the richest iron mines, left $20,000,000. The Duke of Buccleuch (and the Duke of Buccleuch carries half of Scotland in his pocket) left about $30,000,000. The Marquis of Bute was worth, in 1872, about $28,000,000 in land; and he may now be worth $40,000,000 in all. The Duke of Norfolk may be worth $40,000,000, and the Duke of Westminster perhaps $50,000,000." In the United States he gives a list of 70 names representing an aggregate wealth of $2,700,000,-000, an average of more than $37,500,000 each. Although Mr. Shearman, in making this estimate, did not look for less than twenty-millionaires, he discovered incidentally fifty others worth more than $10,000,000 each; and he says that a list of ten persons can be made whose wealth averages $100,000,000; and another list of one hundred persons, whose wealth averages $25,000,000. No such list can be made up in any other country. "The richest dukes of England," he says, "fall below the average wealth of a dozen American citizens; while the greatest bankers, merchants, and railway magnates of England cannot compare in wealth with many Americans."

Mr. Shearman's conclusion is that 25,000 persons own one-half the wealth of the United States; and that the whole wealth of the country is practically owned by 250,000 persons, or one in sixty of the adult male population; and he predicts, from the rapid recent concentration of wealth, that, under present conditions, 50,000 persons will practically own all the wealth of the country in thirty years—or less than one in 500 of the adult male population.

"Sam, why not buy some property, and be a landlord yourself?"

"What's der matter wid yer giving it to me?" said Sam, with a grin. "No," he added, "you can keep yer land. Yer ain't a bad one. Der boys all know about der laying out yer give them fellows at der meeting, and if you was to try to be sociable wid 'em now, they wouldn't be so cold like."

"I don't drink now, and would not ask them to," I answered.

"Smoke?" asked Sam.

ONE OF THE CUSTOMERS.

"No, nor smoke either. I never thought of it before; but the fact is, Sam, I have not smoked since the night you called on me, have had no desire to, and have been so busy that I have not thought of it."

Sam evidently thought it not worth while to answer my last question, and I did not repeat it; but said, as I saw some men crossing the street, evidently making for the bar:

"Sam, how are we to remedy all this? Have you ever thought it out?"

"No," said Sam. "Thet is, another feller thought it out for me, and I read it onct in a paper that was a-pitching inter him, little thinking that by printing what he said fer der purpose of knocking der stuffing out of it, it was really preaching fer der feller, 'cause it caught me right off. 'What a durned fool I am!' I said ter my woman. Well, my woman didn't say nothing; maybe she agreed wid my remark. So I said it over again. 'Yer needn't be telling der children if yer be,' she said. 'Well,' said I, 'here is a feller thet shows me something thet I've been trying ter find out fer ten year, and it's simple as falling off a log: *If any one wants to use the earth, let him pay the rest for the privilege at market rate.* No more fining a feller, like a drunkard or a criminal, fer building a house or painting his barn or being industrious. Jest charge him fer der rent of der land he uses, and thet's all. No more blue-coated pirates ploughing around der coast, wid der new-fangled piratical flag —der American flag wid der stripes running der wrong way! No more locking up all der coal, all der oil, all der gold, all der iron, all der timber, thet God Almighty gave ter us all; but let any feller thet wants ter pay der rest for der privilege, use jest as much as he wants! I warn't such a fool as it seemed at fust, but thet fellow had a big head! You bet your high old muckey muck he's a daisy! He is in it wid both feet, he is. Can't fool him. No siree, bob horse fly! Say, mister, he's der man can explain these things jest as plain as der nose on yer face. Own the land? How in thunder can a man

"A FORGOTTEN WELL."

own land? It was there before he was born, it will be there thousands of years after he has gone, see? Own nothing! I own that thing I showed yer t'other night, 'cause I made it out of der product of der earth; and to prove my ownership, I can destroy it, and no feller can say a word or stop me, see? Like to see yer destroy yer town lot. Guess before yer got ter China, you'd throw up der job; and even if yer did go through ter China, der space would be there all der same, and yer could *sell that space*. Air, thet's all; but it could be bridged over and used, and would bring big money just on account of its being in a town where space is wanted, and lots of people would want to use it. Sell air? Yes; but yer don't own it; yer can't dig thet away, see? Gosh! wouldn't some feller like ter cage up der air, and put a gas-meter on our lungs, and charge us so much a cubic-foot fer air; and if we kicked about der price, they would say, 'Yer needn't be so extravagant. Be economical wid der air: it's ours, and we must be paid for it, see?' Why, they's got a meter in my uncle's cellar in the city that gives away every drop of water he uses. Can't take a drink widout being charged, and if he takes a bath he's got to be rich. His wife takes in washing, and thet water costs her twenty-two dollars every six months. I say, Free Land, Free Water, and Free Labor, them's my sentiments!"

The customers had crossed the street, entered the bar, and were standing waiting to be served, unnoticed by Sam. At the close of his remarks they applauded him and called for their accustomed stimulant; and I left them as they were pouring the fiery stuff down their poor throats.

CHAPTER V.

HE professor came round to the hotel that night highly elated with the success of his day's search for fossils and minerals. All was fish that came to his net—animal, mineral, plant, or fossil—none were strangers to him, and all were of interest; and, better still, he possessed the rare faculty of making them interesting to others. He could sit down by the roadside and talk for an hour over some bit of stone, leaf or plant; and without using one technical term, in every-day language, could tell me more than I can learn in a week's reading; and, what is more to the purpose, I could not only understand him, but remember what he told me. He had the profoundest contempt for collectors of birds' eggs and birds' skins, as a rule, because, as he expressed it, their collections were made like a school-boy's collection of stamps, the owner having all the names pat, and each specimen labeled and numbered, but there it ended. The collection was of no use to the owner or any one else, except for the money value it might possess.

"Now," said the professor, "not to use is to lose. Remember that, my boy, and if you

"THE MOON IS ALL RIGHT."

get a good idea from any of your old books, write it down, repeat it to the first man that you can make listen to you; nab a small boy, your sister, mother, brother, servant, car-driver or policeman, and give him or her your idea. They may not appreciate it, may not be interested in it, may not understand it. What of that? By repeating it to them, you are using it. By writing it down and sending it to the publisher or a friend, you are using it; by using it you are making it *your own*, and no one can take it from you. You have added to your stock, you have added to your education, you have added to your ability for use in this world; and the man who presumes to live on this grand planet, and does not endeavor to be of use, practically denies the existence of a God, practically denies that he owes anything to mankind—in fact,

PROF. FOLLIUM.

by so living, insolently and boldly affirms that he is above God and man.

"Now, these collectors are not so bad as that; they are of some use; their collections, sooner or later, are sold, and go to enrich some museum; but they have not repaid the collector for his work because he was satisfied with the selfish pleasure of possessing a better or more complete collection than some other fellow, and with knowing the names and being able to repeat them like a parrot. If you collect books, read them; and when you leave this world, see to it that your collection goes to some library, where the books belong, and not to heirs, whose only interest is in the money your bequest will bring at an auction. Never buy a book because it is rare. You are not a dealer; buy only such books as are of use to you in your particular line of thought or are necessary to perfect your collection, for its ultimate place on the shelves of some public institution, where others interested in the same line of study may find them.

"Hello! Where did you get this?" said the professor, as his eyes lighted upon the bookshelf, and he made a dive for an old book on botany. "Well, here is a prize," said he, as he opened the book. "I have tried all the book-stalls in London in search of this volume and have never met with it before"; and after rubbing his glasses with his silk handkerchief, the professor replaced them on his nose, and without waiting for a reply, commenced to pore over the volume, and was soon lost to all surroundings.

This was not exactly what I expected. I wanted to talk. I wanted him to combat the ideas I had just received from Sam; but it must have been an hour before the little man looked up, and the expression of humility and chagrin that spread over his face was comical, as he stammered out an apology for forgetting my presence and where he was. He closed the book, looked it over, the brass-clasp binding and all, carefully replaced it on the shelf, and said:

"Well, what do you intend to do? Go into tenement-house reform? Start a Cooper's Institute? Build a hospital, or run for Congress? There is a great field in the tenement-house—sanitary plumbing, more light, parks, water on each floor, house rules, and all that sort of thing, you know."

"Yes," I replied, "I've thought of that, but what then? My tenement-house would be a flat, and would be occupied by the middle classes, so-called, because the rents would be too high for the people for whom it was built."

"True enough," replied he, "but why charge such high rent?"

"Because I would be compelled to. There is a market value for such flats, and the price is fixed. Should I lower it, I would in reality be giving in alms the difference between my charge and the market value, and those who accept alms cannot do so without injury to their manhood and independence. I would either fill my house with what are popularly known as dead-beats, or I would make paupers of men, who before, though poor, were self-sustaining."

"My dear fellow," laughed the professor, "you have made wonderful progress in a very short time!"

"For which, in a great measure, I am indebted to a bar-keeper," I replied, at the same time remembering Sam's cutting remarks about the conscience-money and the hospitals and public institutions. I related these remarks to the professor, and he was mightily pleased, and laughed until the tears dimmed his glasses.

"Well, run your mines on the co-operative plan, then," he said, as soon as he regained his composure.

"No, I cannot do that either; because by so doing I would only be enriching a comparatively few miners and doing nothing to change the system. The immediate effect would be to make a position in my mines worth so much premium, and the needy would all sell out to get ready money for present necessities; while the ultimate end would be that the benefit would fall upon those among the miners (or those who might have become miners) who were already comparatively well off. Possibly I would have an efficient set of workmen, but it would be practically only enlarging a company by taking in so many more stockholders, and the principle would remain the same. The poor degraded slaves I see about me would still be poor degraded slaves. Neither could I sell my mines or give them away, because that would be merely shirking a responsibility—an attempt to shove it upon some one else's shoulders. I have thought of all that."

"I see you have, my boy, and thought of it more deeply than I ever did, I must ac-

knowledge. Now, I can plainly see that a
fellow of your pluck will not try to shirk
either a fight or a responsibility, and you
have both ahead of you, for all other mine
owners will bitterly oppose any suggestions
from you, and fiercely resent any reforms
you may choose to introduce in your own
mines. Not only that, but they will have the
public on their side—the great, unthinking
booby called the public, that is plundered,
robbed, insulted, and imposed upon in a manner that any individual fragment of it in the
form of a man would resent instantly if the
insult or imposition were put upon him personally as separated from the rest. Why, it
is amusing to see the public in New York
driven about like cattle by creatures living
upon its own permission. I mean the corporations whose charters are granted by the
public, whose money comes from the public,
whose valuable franchises are rendered valuable by the public, but who, one and all, by
their every act, word, and speech, claim to
own the public whose servants they ought
and were originally intended to be. They
make rules of their own, in defiance of the
comforts or rights of the public, and enforce
them as laws, and the great, stupid public

accepts them as such. I tell you, a man cannot travel from the Battery to Harlem without having every particle of manhood in him trampled upon. There, I've said what has been on my mind for a long time, and in repeating it, according to my own precepts, have made it my own, I suppose," said the professor.

Well, it was my turn to laugh then. I could see, without the aid of my spiritual eyes, that the professor had been badly used in the great city; but I seldom saw anything else than the real man in my learned friend; and, as was the case with Sam, I never found it necessary to use my newly acquired powers to read him as I would a book, because both men were strictly honest and made no attempt to conceal their real selves, which were so plainly discernible in their speech and looks.

There was a knock at my door, and "Humpy," or Nate as I now called him, answered my summons to come in.

"Your superintendent is down stairs, sir, and wishes to see you immediately."

"Send him up, Nate," said I. "No, professor, don't leave; nothing private—something in regard to mines," I continued as I saw my friend knocking the ashes from his pipe, preparatory to leaving.

"Come right in, Clint," I called, as I heard my mine superintendent's heavy tread outside. "Come in. Mr. Butts, Professor Follium."

The two men shook hands, and, as they stood there, the contrast was striking; the round, intelligent head of the professor bearing the marks of refinement, culture and good nature in every curved line from the top of his round bald head to the bottom of his round bald chin, in direct contrast to my superintendent's not less intelligent but less refined appearance.

CLINT BUTTS, MY SUPERINTENDENT.

Clint Butts was a large, square man, with

a broad, square forehead, a heavy, square jaw; his brows were two broad, straight, dark lines separated by twin vertical wrinkles; his gray eyes were deep-set, with long black lashes, his nose was very regular and straight, and his dark, closely cropped mustache ran in almost a horizontal line beneath it. As if he was conscious of nature's attempt in the rectangular plan and had a desire to help her out, Clint wore a square-cut, double-breasted sack coat and heavy-soled, square-toed shoes. Immense reserve force both of mind and body, was the impression Clint Butts made upon any one whom he met. An iron will and great physical endurance were expressed in every line of his face and figure. Honesty with him was a matter of course; he could not round off his sharp corners with any sort of deception, and this trait made him both dreaded and respected by miner and mine owner. If Clint was asked for an opinion, he gave it without fear or favor; if ordered by his employer to do anything, he did it without words, so when he turned to me after greeting the professor I knew I would soon be master of the facts, whatever they were, that caused his visit.

"Sit down, Clint, and tell me what's up. Anything wrong at the mines?" I inquired.

"There is going to be a strike for an advance in wages."

"Humph! What do the men get now?" I asked. "You know," I explained, feeling ashamed of my ignorance, "I never did understand the wage system; fact is, I never bothered myself about these matters of detail until the conference was called, and I am not yet up on all the points; but I have an impression that the men make about two dollars a day, when they work."

"That seems to be the general impression of the public; but I am sorry to say that the men seldom, if ever, make such a sum. The wage system in the anthracite-coal region is a complicated affair, and each complication deprives the miner of more or less money. With the 'sliding scale,' as it is sometimes called, or 'basis system,' as we call it, the wages of the miner fluctuate with the price of coal. We call it the basis system because the market price of coal is the basis upon which the miner's wages are paid."

"Mr. Butts, this is very interesting," said the professor, beaming through his glasses; "and it strikes me as not an unwise arrangement, if I understand aright. When there is a rise in coal, there is a corresponding rise in the wages of the miners; and if there should be a sudden drop in the market price of coal, the corresponding drop in the wages paid the men would in a measure prevent the owners from a great loss which, being unlooked for, might be disastrous."

"True," replied Clint; "but so many abuses have been forced in the system that the basis system has become one of the most oppressive tools in the hands of owners."

"How is that, Clint? What are the abuses? Come, let us have the whole story," said I, as I handed Clint a pipe and a pouch of tobacco. The pipe he declined but accepted the proffered tobacco, and filled his own odd-looking French clay pipe. In lighting the tobacco he made that loud smacking noise with his lips, peculiar to Irishmen.

"The professor here knows something of the manner in which coal is prepared for the market," continued Clint, "for I saw him examining our breakers. He saw how the coal was crushed between two big revolving cylinders, toothed with steel, and afterward saw how the coal was run through screens, where it was assorted into the several sizes from 'broken' pieces, which are as large as an ordinary tea-cup, to what is called 'buckwheat,' which is, in plain language, dirt. Then we have 'lump' coal, which comes a little larger than 'broken.' Now you see, gentlemen," continued Clint, and he held the pipe between his fingers and blew a cloud of smoke before the sentence, "when the basis sytem was first established there were but six grades of coal sold in the market, namely, lump, steamboat, broken, egg, stove and chestnut. These were all high-priced grades—"

"What's that got to do with the abuses?" I said a little impatiently; for these details were still rather dry to me in spite of my efforts to understand them all.

"Just this," replied Clint: "Lately two lower grades of coal have been added to the list and one higher grade, steamboat, dropped. Now, according to the basis, miners in this anthracite-coal district receive

42½ cents for cutting and loading a ton of coal when the market price is $5. Out of this 42½ cents they must pay 'help,' and pay a profit to the mine owner at the company's store, on the powder, oil, fuse and all the other incidental expenses of a miner's work, besides the dockage—"

"What is the dockage?" I inquired.

"Deductions made by the docking boss for slate, light loading, or any other cause that may suggest itself to him; and, as his living depends upon what he knocks off the miners' earnings, you may be sure he will not fail to find a cause for dockage—and this notwithstanding the fact that the men mine thirteen extra cubic feet to the ton to cover these very deficiencies.

"Coal has not been quoted as high as $5 since 1875. This would make the consumers who pay $6 and $6.25 per ton open their eyes, but it is true, and this is the way it is arranged. As I said before, at the start of the basis system there were but six grades of coal, all high-priced ones. Now there are seven, and two of them are low-priced grades. If you will just run over this table," said Clint, "you will see what I mean."

THE TABLE.

1 Lump Coal	$6.00	Lump	$6.00
2 Steamboat	5.00	Broken	5.00
3 Broken	5.00	Egg	5.50
4 Egg	5.50	Stove	5.00
5 Stove	5.00	Chestnut	3.50
6 Chestnut	3.50	Pea, new grade	2.00
		Buckwheat, new grade	1.25
	6 | 30.00		7 | 28.25
Average	5.00	*Average	4.03¾

* EXTRACT FROM LETTER TO NEW YORK PAPER BY T. V. POWDERLY.

When it is published that an anthracite-coal miner receives so much money for one day's work, it causes men, in New York as well as in Wisconsin, to believe that he ought not to grumble at short time now and then. But his expenses are never set forth, in fact I have never seen a reference to them in print; everything goes to show that he draws from $5 to $8 a day. Let us say that a full month consists of twenty-five days. The miner gets out seven cars a day, and at the end of the month his account will stand this way:

```
25 full days—175 cars..........................$153.12
    Out of which he pays:
Laborer at the rate of $2.10 a day..............$52.50
Powder at $3 a keg..............................  36.00
Dockage for month...............................   9.62
Smithing for month..............................    .65
Oil for lamp....................................   2.00
Cotton for lampwick.............................    .20
Squibs to ignite powder.........................    .30
Waterproof paper................................    .25
Soap for mining purposes........................    .05
Wear and tear on tools for month................    .75

Total expenses for month......................$102.32

Which deduct from.............................$153.12

Leaves him as result of month's toil..........  $50.80
```

From the foregoing statement it will be seen that with a full

"Thus you see how the wages are reduced by forcing the miners to accept two new grades of coal; and, mind you, gentlemen, these last two grades are made from the dirt and waste that the miner *has already been docked for*. He is a fortunate miner who can clear a dollar a day; and even he must spend that dollar at the company's store and in rent to the company for the house he lives in, and thus it all goes back to the mine owner."

month's work the miner will have over and above his expenses but $50.80. The Hampton is an ordinary mine and is operated by the D., L. and W. Company. The best mine, so miners tell me, owned by that Company, is the Central. Both Hampton and Central shafts are in the limits of Scranton, on what is called the Hyde Park side of the city. In the Central the miner is paid at the rate of $1.07½ per car, gets out six cars for a day's work when mining bottom coal and eight cars when mining top coal. Top coal is easiest to mine.

ANOTHER BALANCE SHEET.

Computing the earnings of the miner at bottom coal prices it will leave him but from $8 to $10 more in the month than is paid in the other mine. Giving the miner his full month's wages at top coal prices, or at the rate of eight cars a day, and he will receive $8.60 per day and a total of $215 for the month. Out of this he pays:

For laborer	$60.00
Powder	20.00
Dockage	9.00
Oil for lamp	2.00
Other expenses same as in other mine	2.25
Total	$93.25
Leaving a balance for the miner of	$121.75

If a miner were allowed to work top-coal during the month, that

"Pitch right in, Clint; don't mind me. I am getting used to the position of slave-driver and robber, and don't mind it, I assure you; but I want facts now. Tell us what some one miner you know makes a day," I interrupted.

"There is Nathaniel James," answered Clint. "For the last two weeks' work he received $8.50, or $4.25 per week. This is the best that could be done in the anthracite mines. The miner works bottom coal for a distance and then takes down the top-coal, so it will be seen that he must take the chance when it comes to him, and that chance is given to but a very few. I have not heard of a case in which such a month's work was performed, and for years no miner has made full time. The best average earnings of this region for the past year will not exceed $30 per month. I have placed the expenses for powder, dockage, wear and tear and supplies at the lowest figure.

A COMMON OCCURRENCE.

Up to to-day, Feb. 27th, the Sloan shaft has worked but two days. The miner, after paying his laborer and other expenses, will take home to his family not more than $6 for this month, unless the last day of the month is worked. The best time made in any of the mines around here this month will not exceed six days, and the miner will not make over $14 for the month. For the last year and a half times have been poor, some months almost as bad as this and others but a trifle better.

WHAT A PICTURE OF POVERTY!

Imagine what the fare must be of a family that is depending on $6 a month. Economists, those who advise workingmen to practise economy, should do as I did last Wednesday evening— eat supper with a miner who had nothing on the table for his family of seven but cornmeal mush and water.

man is a steady, industrious man and one of the most practical miners of the middle coal fields. Nate never tastes a drop of liquor and never loses a day's work except for sickness, or some such urgent cause. He is the father of the little humpback boot-black at the hotel, and 'Humpy' owes his name and hump to an accident in the mines when he was almost an infant. Nate told me the other day that his earnings, not counting Humpy's, amounted to just 15 cents a day, divided *per capita* among his family. Now here is a report," continued Clint, taking a pamphlet from his pocket, "showing the cost of maintaining paupers at the present time to be 28 cents per day for each pauper; that is, your best miners' families are living on just a little over half what it costs the county to keep a pauper!"

"Lord!" said the professor, "I knew things were bad, yes, extremely bad; but goodness me! I had no idea they were so horribly bad as your figures make them out to be, Mr. Butts. It seems to me," said the man of science, "that a knowledge of mathematics would make paupers of all the miners, or else cause them to kill their babies as fast as they were born."

"It makes tramps of some," continued Clint. "If you at any time want to know what wages the miners are receiving, watch the newspapers closely, and you will see reported the fact that a few men meet monthly in New York City and arbitrarily set the figures at which coal is to be sold. Now make a table of these figures like the one I have just shown you, strike your average, and use this proportion: As the original $5.00 a ton is to the 42½ cents, so is the average you have struck to the wages of the miners at the time the quotations were made. Simple Rule of Three, you see. For instance, if coal sells now at $4.00, the miner will receive a little over 34 cents for mining a ton. Remember that a good miner and his help can cut about ten tons a day; help costs $2.10 per day, and that one keg of powder costs $2.75, and will cut from twenty-five to thirty tons of coal, and dockage will average six per cent. of all coal sent out; and don't forget that all miners' supplies come from the company's store and at extortionate prices."

"That will do for to-night, Clint. I have as much on my conscience as it will bear at present. Why have you never told me this before?" I asked; but I saw the answer before Clint gave it, and hastened to forestall him with "That's all right; I understand." Then I asked: "What advance will my men ask for, and when?"

"They will ask, as my informant tells me, for the abolition of the two cheap or dirt coals from the list, and a restoration of steamboat, and will not make the demand until next week."

"How do you get your information, Clint?"

"From a Pinkerton who belongs to their society, and reports to me once a week."

"Have the men announced it publicly as yet, or has it leaked out, that there will be a strike?"

"No, sir."

"Then cause a notice to be posted immediately, commending the men for their faithfulness—I have been watching them at work and at home, and I must confess that I was more than surprised at the general industry and economy of these poor fellows—and end it with a proclamation to the effect that on and after date an increase of ten per cent. will be given. We will retain the system because I think that by gradually eliminating the evils, it may be made a good thing. By the way, Clint, if these fellows had free use of the land around here, could they make $2.00 a day?"

The answer came promptly, "Yes, sir; with half the work they do now, and every day in the week."

"That will do, Clint. See that the notice is posted."

Clint rose, and looked at me in a curious sort of way, but said nothing.

"Did you hear?" I continued. "Give the poor fellows an advance of ten per cent.— no, make it fifteen—and some compliment on their industry thrown in, and do it before they make a formal demand — forestall them—do you see?"

"I understand, sir," answered the superintendent. "You know what that means?"

"Why, it means more money for the poor wretches."

"Yes, sir," answered the practical man of facts, "it means that and more. It means that you will precipitate a strike through the whole coal region; it means that all the other corporations and private owners will be down on you and combine against

AS THE MOON WATCHED THE OLD CONTINENTAL FREEZING AT VALLEY FORGE.

you ; that your coal will be boycotted by the railroads. It means a fight!"*

"Well, Clint, are n't you game for a fight?"

Clint's broad mouth widened still further into a broader smile, as he answered, " You are the boss, sir. If you know what the step you are taking means, and will see me through, I rather guess I'm game enough to carry out my part of the job. I'd rather face the corporations than the Mollies, and I've faced *them* in some pretty ticklish situations. Good night, sir." And Clint bowed himself out.

* EXTRACT FROM A LETTER TO THE "STANDARD.'

Away back in the 70's Mr. Coxe was a land owner, having all his collieries except Drifton (his home) leased to outside parties, who operated them. In the spring of 1877 the coal trade reached its lowest ebb, the mine workers worked six or eight days per month, and Mr. Coxe realized the necessity of seeking wider markets for anthracite coal. He surveyed the field and called his men together, making the proposition that if they agreed to work at a specified rate of wages for said year he would warrant them steady work for that period. The men accepted, and Mr. Coxe commenced operations by building boats and shipping coal by the lakes into the western market. He was a pioneer in the business, and expended an enormous sum to make the enterprise a success.

In the meantime the Lehigh Valley railroad company had its secret agents at work buying up and grabbing all available coal lands. In a short time the Lehigh Valley company, in direct violation of the state constitution, commenced operations as miners

"You are in for it now," said the professor. "But from the looks of your superintendent, I think you have a good man to back you; and if you will make a place at your office for your friend the bar-keeper, you three will form a strong combination of talent. Of all men, a bar-keeper has the greatest opportunities of knowing other men's weak points, and this barkeeper appears to have intelligence enough to make use of his knowledge. Good night and good luck to you! I leave in the morning on the early train. I am sorry, for I should dearly like to see you through this. Good-bye."

and shippers of coal, and of course coveted Mr. Coxe's western market. For a while competition was keen, but Mr. Coxe, being an energetic business man, and having a fair field, was amply able to hold his own. He was compelled to ship his coal over the Lehigh Valley road, and the company determined to exterminate him by discriminations in tolls. Mr. Coxe, after appealing in vain to other individual operators for aid and co-operation, went it alone and brought the Valley company before the inter-state commerce commissioners, with the result that that august body has failed to render a decision, although the case has been in their hands for three years.

In the meantime Mr. Coxe's leases have expired, all his mines being controlled and operated by himself. He is a land user and as hopelessly in the grasp of the railroads as his poor miners are in his. But he does not stop here. He is building a railroad of his own to connect with four trunk-lines, apparently ignoring the fact that these four roads may pool their issues and leave him more helpless and dependent than before.

Once again I was left alone in the room with the fishing-rods, guns, and weird books of that mysterious regular boarder ; but the

"THE OLD, WHITE-FACED MOON SAW THIS."

fire burned brightly and from the outside the moon peeped into the window, with a face as broad and determined-looking as my superintendent's. No wonder, poor thing! If it has any heart at all, it must be worn out or hardened to flint by the sights it sees as it sails through the clouds that surround our poor, wicked, blind, and ignorant little earth.

I wondered if, at the birth of this nation, as the moon watched "the old Continentals in their ragged regimentals," starving and freezing at Valley Forge, it had any hopes of seeing the spirit of freedom that these heroes were suffering for, triumph; or if its lunar experience in watching other like struggles, which were crushed in the end by the very wealth the temporary freedom created, taught it to foresee a like end to the old Continentals' hopes.

Freedom is health: slavery is disease. And even while our ancestors were suffering from the surgical operation that cut out the cancer of monarchy, they left, as an inheritance for their children, a pustule called negro slavery. The old, white-faced moon saw this—saw the disease grow until it proved almost fatal; and the silver light from the sky shone over many a bloody field where Labor laid on the altar of Freedom thousands of her sons.

Yes, and as we were resting after that almost fatal operation of the surgeon's painful knife, the old moon saw, and still sees, another neoplasm forming on Uncle Sam's body. All of these diseases come from the roots of the old monarchical cancer left in the nation's system.

James Henry Hammond voiced the sentiments of the old Slave States when he said:

"In all social systems there must be a class to do the mean duties, to perform the drudgery of life; that is, a class requiring but a low order of intellect and but little skill. Its requisites are vigor, docility, fidelity. Such a class you must have, or you would not have that other class which leads progress, refinement, and civilization. It constitutes the very mudsills of society and of political government; and you might as well attempt to build a house in the air as to build either the one or the other except on the mudsills. Fortunately for the South, she found a race adapted to that purpose to her hand—a race inferior to herself, but eminently qualified in temper, in vigor, in docility, in capacity to stand the climate, to answer all her purposes."

And this old believer in chattel slavery was right, when, continuing, he said:

"We use them for the purpose and call them slaves. We are old-fashioned at the South yet; it is a word discarded now by ears polite; but I will not characterize that class at the North with that term; but you have it; it is there; it is everywhere!"

Mudsills! Ah, the poor mudsills upon which all our wealth and power rest! What if these mudsills, after a drenching rain, should become slippery? What if they should slide? What becomes of the temples, churches, and cities, whose massive walls rest so heavily on the earth as to cause a landslide? The broad-faced moon knows. She has seen them dashed to pieces, in one confused mass; she has seen old Mother Nature heal up the wound and hide the scar with wild flowers, trees and vines; and the earth still rolled on!

"O thou ghostly phantom of the sky that hast watched our puny, selfish race for so many centuries, tell me," I cried, "are we to be another Rome? Is our glorious republic to be sacrificed because the rich are insatiable and the poor are slaves?"

"Not by a long shot!" answered a voice

in anything but a lunar tone. "We're all
right," continued the voice, which I at once
recognized to be Sam's. " Don't you see der
moon's all right, too? Thet's what she
means by squinting thet left eye. She says,
says she, ' Yer don't build no fence around
me. Yer can't stick yer trespass signs up
on me. I'm a free-trader, a free-thinker, a
free-lander. I goes booming right along
'bout my business, and a millionaire ain't no
more to me than nothing ; I don't know 'em ;
they hain't in it, and hain't got a jewel in
their hoard that can shine like me. I'm all
right. I'm in the push, I am! I'm the poor
man's gas-company, and never send a man
'round to pertend to read the meter, and
charge him so much a cubic-foot for moon-
light. No, sir-ree bob horse fly ; what I've
got, I give, and ask no questions. I'm a
white man, I am. I'm a true democrat thet's
just as happy a letting my 'light shine ' on
a lot of innocent niggers in ' darkest Africa '
as I am shining on a lot of poor dudes stag-
gering home from der club. I don't blame
der dudes : they can't help being born rich,
and I don't consider it any more disgrace than
being born in der top of a tenement house
or in a Spring Valley coal miner's hut after

der mortgage was foreclosed by der wealthy men who ran that bunco game.'"

"Hold on, Sam!" I shouted, laughing, "hold on! The moon doesn't use any such slangy speech as that."

"No," answered Sam, with a grin, "no more 'n she does poetry. To a feller who only talks slang, the moon expresses herself in slang. To the poetry chap, the moon is poetical; to me, the moon is democratical."

Sam was about to pass on his way through the hall, when I called to him, and told him of the conversation between the superintendent and myself, and of the fight in prospect. At the word "fight," Sam set down his bad-smelling lamp that he had been holding in one hand, and protecting from the draught with the other.

A smile like that which had broadened the mouth of my superintendent caused Sam's kinky moustache to curl at the ends, and he slid into a chair near the door, and waited for further details. I told him what the professor had said, and that, as Mr. Keene would say, "it coincided with my preconceived ideas exactly."

Sam's face looked solemn in an instant, and he was about to decline my proffer of a position. I saw it was because he thought it was made for him out of a sort of charitable feeling. I hastened to explain how useful he would be to me, and then I met another unlooked-for opposition in regard to the amount he was to receive for his services.

"No, sir," he said, "'tain't no use talking. I ain't wuth any such sum as thet ; and while I would, if I could, demand as my right every durned cent I am wuth, to take a cent more is to acknowledge myself to myself as a pauper or a parasite living off some one else."

At last I let the matter of salary drop; and he consented to accept the situation, emoluments to be agreed upon after trial, provided I would allow him to do the square thing by the hotel man and get another fellow to fill his place as clerk and bar-keeper, etc.; and I bade him good-night.

Not long after engaging Sam as a private secretary and general assistant I received notice that the regular boarder was expected to return and claim possession of his room ; and having succeeded in finding a man from a neighboring town to take Sam's place at the bar, and a small Italian to assume Nate's duties of sweep, bootblack, and bell-boy, our little colony decided to move from the straggling, dirty mining town to a no less dirty and hopeless-looking spot in the vicinity of my own mines, which were situated some eight or ten miles distant.

When we arrived, we were received by Mr. Butts at the depot, and escorted to our quarters. Clint had erected for me a snug little shanty, with an office in front and a bedroom in the rear. The village, if the group of shanties adjoining my mines could be dignified by such a name, I christened "Moonblight."

CHAPTER VI.

NOT many months after we had settled in our new quarters, while I was busy working over plans and studying out some new schemes, the door flew open and in came a muffled figure. Above the fur collar of the overcoat gleamed a pair of gold-rimmed glasses, and a moment later I was grasping the hand of Professor Follium.

"Well, now, this is snug!" exclaimed the little man, as he looked around at the scattered paper, architects' plans, surveyors' implements, top-boots, axes, picks, patent lamps, models, and all the medley of material that a few months had collected around me. "But where on earth did you find such a name for your city?" inquired the professor, as his eye caught a new, colored plan of the village, laid out and mapped under the directions of Clinton Butts, C. E.

"Oh, it's a long story, Professor," I replied; "but I feel like talking, for I have done very little of it lately. I have not had time to talk much since I saw you last. I will tell you all about it; but first tell me where you came from, and what brought you away out here this time of the year?"

"Never mind about me. My doings are uninteresting. Been on a lecturing tour; was in the neighborhood, and my curiosity to know how you were getting on, added to my desire to see you, made me time my engagements so that I might have a few days off when I reached this neighborhood; and, now I am here, I am anxious to know what possessed you to choose such a queer name for your proposed city—for I see by Mr. Butts's map here that you intend to make a city of it. Please tell me what that word means, where you got it, and how you came to choose it. I am as curious as a child." And throwing himself back on the wolf-skin that covered an easy-chair near the open fire, the professor assumed a comfortable attitude of attention. There was a twinkle in his eye, as he glanced at my long, curly hair and blond beard, but he made no remarks upon them.

I began and told him my whole experience during the night spent with those strange books of the "regular boarder" at the American House. During the recital the pleasant face of my friend assumed as grave a look as it was possible for muscles accustomed to be stimulated only by dry good humor, mirth and good-fellowship to assume: when I finished he remained silent for a long time, and then muttered:

"Remarkable!

A SKETCH FROM NATURE.

remarkable! Why, you are a regular St. Paul!" he exclaimed at last, as his face regained its accustomed good-natured expression. "But do you know," he continued, "I believe that both you and St. Paul were unconsciously preparing yourselves for the change that was to come, long before the light blinded you. Had your mind not been prepared you would not have understood the message when it came; the old book of magic would have been simply an old book of magic—nothing more. The deeper meaning was in you, or the book could not have reached you. With most of us this change is so gradual that we are unconscious of it. If our spiritual eyes are opened, it is by such slow degrees that we do not know it, and attribute our insight into hidden things to an accomplishment acquired by constant practice in looking for the real meaning of what we see.

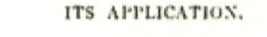
ITS APPLICATION.

So you found Mr. Keene to be a fox and a wolf? Ha, ha!" laughed the little fellow. "And that spider illustration—why! that's an inspiration. I have a collection of those spiders at the college, and I'll never look at them again without thinking of your mine owners' meeting. Oh, they are financiers, those spiders! They live, literally, in a bed of roses and grow fat on the blood of the industrious bees. Good! Grand! I'll use that illustration in my next lecture, if I am mobbed for it; and if I can find that regular boarder, I'll pawn my clothes to buy his witch-book. But first I will try to 'purify my mind.'" And again the grave look chased the dimples from the rosy cheek of the man of science. "Yes, sir; I'll become an alchemist too, and try to see how much gold I can make out of my audiences. No pun, no pun; I did not mean it that way. You cannot get much money out of people when you want to teach them anything: they will pay to be amused, but as a rule, they hate to be instructed. It makes them think, and if they think, why, then, my dear boy, they might see things as they really are, eh?"

"Professor," I exclaimed, "you do not

know how pleasant it is to hear you talk like this! I was certain that you would not laugh at me—at least, I thought I was; but the relief I feel at hearing you indorse my opinions and approve my actions shows me that there must have been a lurking fear or doubt that you would, like the villagers in the other town, think that I was flighty; and while, generally, such things do not bother me, I would have felt it grievously if you too had harbored any such thought. I may yet have need of your testimony as an expert; for Mr. Keene has twice tried to cause my arrest and incarceration as a lunatic. I have been shadowed by detectives—my steps dogged by agents of the combination of Keene, White, and Brown. Even my long hair and beard were urged by my enemies as signs of insanity. In vain have Keene, White, and Brown searched for my heirs, hoping that they would cause me to be locked up as incompetent to take care of my estate. I knew, if they found them, they would do more than I can do, for I am the last of our line in this country, and the other branches are all across the water, bearing a different name. The name I am known by is one assumed by an old ancestor when he escaped to this country from the political persecution in England to which his outspoken ideas on government subjected him; hence I feel comparatively easy on that score."

"They think, or pretend to think, you a lunatic? Ah, the rogues! It would be well for them, and for the poor wretches upon

"I AM A FIRM BELIEVER IN GNOMES, BROWNIES, AND FAIRIES AS REAL LIVE BEINGS."

whose labor they live, if your lunacy were contagious. I shall add a new word to my dictionary: 'Moonblight—That sort of lunacy that causes a man to try to act like a man'; and I will change the definition of 'financiering' to 'That sort of lunacy which makes a man forget that he is a man'; and every time that I find among my collection of old prints the picture of a witch on a broom, I'll draw around her head one of those hoops or pin-wheels such as the old masters always put around the heads of saints. As for your beard and hair, why, they make you positively handsome; they are nature's own adornment. Not only

"I AM A FIRM BELIEVER IN GNOMES, BROWNIES, AND FAIRIES AS REAL LIVE BEINGS."

have you taught me, my boy, to believe in the old books of magic, but I have already taken a step ahead of you. I am a firm believer in gnomes, brownies, and fairies as real live beings. I mean it—I believe in them.

"An artist conceives a great picture before he has drawn a line or put a brush to the canvas; and so real is it that he will alter the composition, take a figure out here, and put one in there; and yet, to all the world but the painter, that picture is invisible. A poet will conceive a poem while the paper before him is blank and his pen dry. An architect will build a palace, and frequently select designs for minor details of ornament, while it is still a castle in the air, visible only to the architect himself. An inventor makes a machine while vainly trying to sleep at night, surrounded by darkness and dressed in his night-clothes, and nothing is visible to any one's sight but his own until he embodies his thoughts in wood or iron. All these things are real. Who can deny their existence? They are the gnomes, the brownies, the fairies, wearing their magical caps which render them invisible. When the caps are removed, we see pictures, poems, buildings, operas or machinery—whatever excites our admiration, veneration, and wonder.

"There is not a principle in government that did not first have its existence in the mind of some dreamer or 'crank.' There is not a reform accomplished that did not originate as an immaterial, intangible thing called a thought. Each human being is constantly conjuring up and sending forth innumerable fairies, gnomes and brownies, to caper around the earth, performing all sorts of mischievous, vicious, harmless, pleasant, entertaining, helpful, or useful acts; and these little folks never die, but go capering on through all time, bobbing up here and there, in the most unexpected and surprising manner.

"Everything that represents the product of human labor first existed as a thought, and without the application of human labor, which removed the magical cap, would have died a thought, unknown and unseen by the world. What is true of us is true of nature. Every object, plant, mountain, river, sea, continent, must first have existed as a thought."

"Yes, professor, I too believe in the fairies you describe, and these little folk give me courage; these are the fairies that supported me when, in spite of my wealth, I felt helpless and incapable of doing aught to alleviate the suffering I saw around me. Whether the reforms I have introduced at my mines will of themselves result in good, I know not; but this much I can see with my spiritual eyes—that an honest, thoughtful effort for the good of others, in spite of mistakes and blunders, never fails to result in good. I think that there are many rough diamonds among my men, who need only the jeweler to make them gems of great value."

"Gems?" interrupted the lecturer; "the soil of the road, farm, or barnyard, when crystallization has rearranged the molecules, is worn by us as ornaments of the greatest value, and we hoard them in our treasure chests or place them behind the locks and bars of a safe-deposit vault for safe keeping; yet, day by day, we trample the same material under foot or carefully brush it from our clothes, and call it dirt. We never think of how much greater value it is in the form of dirt, the food-supply for all vegetation! That is not impromptu; it is from my last lecture, but it applies here, so I use it.

"Suppose that all the different molecules that go to compose the so-called precious stones were allowed to assume the form of crystals. With diamonds enough to build our houses, we should die of starvation. You could not farm land composed of diamonds; the hardiest plant could receive no nourishment if planted in a bed of rubies; corn would not grow in a field of emeralds.

All vegetation would cease to exist for want of food and all animal life would soon follow from the same cause. Neither animals nor vegetables can live on gems."

"Professor," I interrupted, "there is a gem whose crystallization cannot hurt it; it is love — the only thing of real value in this world; and usefulness is another name for love. Here, I have discovered, is the secret cause of the nobility that made the humpback's face shine the morning after the memorable night spent with the old books, in the regular boarder's room. Nate's only thought is for others; his own fate, discomfort or inconvenience never adds weight to the burden his poor, distorted back has to bear."

But the little man had warmed up to his lecture, and apparently without heeding the interruption, continued:

"Dirt is of inestimable value, as it represents the love of the Creator in providing a storehouse from which his creatures are to get their food, clothing, and shelter. Nature, through the medium of wild plants and animals, prepares the crude material in a form fit for the support and shelter of man; but man cannot obtain it without labor. Man, even in his most primitive state, must labor as a hunter and fisherman to live."

The professor gave me many points which, from my lack of scientific education, I should have missed. He directed my attention to the fact that physical force became an element in society when the primitive man discovered that weapons he used to kill game would kill his brother as well, and employed those weapons to compel his weaker, or not so well-armed, brother to hunt and fish for him.

"Yes," said my friend, "he risked his life and that of his family and tribe for the chance of living upon the labor of others."

"But he was a savage," said I.

"Ah, yes; and that gnome, conjured up by the primitive savage, still lives. He and slavery were born together, and will exist together until physical force ceases to control, and usefulness has the seat of honor. The gnome conjured up by the primitive man, and made visible by the use of weapons against his brother savage, is the gnome that builds our forts, that plans our ironclads, that drills our armies, and sits alongside the banker and railroad magnate in the counting-room and in the office. This last, my dear fellow, is impromptu, and *not* in my lecture."

"Bravo!" I exclaimed. "There is nothing like science to help a fellow, either in speechmaking or in a mining operation."

I do not remember a morning spent more enjoyably than that winter morning in the office of my shanty at Moonblight.

I had a large open fire, and although coal was everywhere, I burned wood. It is so cheerful and bright, and then the smell of it takes me back to the old homestead in Ohio where I lived as a boy. This wood-fire was the only real luxury in which I indulged. The furniture of the office was made by the carpenter, and the easy-chair that the professor occupied, had it not been for the wolf-skin carriage-robe thrown over it, would have been but a hard seat; for it was made of pine boards in a very primitive manner. Like a couple of boys, we two sat there in front of the fire, and took turns poking the logs, to see the sparks go up the chimney, and we talked as fast as any two school-chums when they meet after their holiday vacation.

"Come," said the professor, "tell me all about your plans and what you have done."

"As I have told you, my steps at first were

dogged, and I was everywhere shadowed by detectives. You informed me when last I saw you that I was 'in for it,' and I *am* in for it, heart and soul. Thanks to the book of Magus, I can read men, and I recognized these spies at a glance; but at first I had the greatest difficulty in restraining Sam, whose indignation would get the better of his universal-peace doctrine; and both he and Clint were bent on 'doing' the detectives."

"'Doing' them?" said the professor. "I do not quite understand."

"Oh, it is one of Sam's expressions, and means pounding and jumping on them until they are good subjects for the hospital. Sam is invaluable, always bright and ready for what the day may bring forth. He believes that physical force is wrong, and if his indignation should get the better of him at any time, and cause him to knock a man down, he would be abject in his apologies the next moment. Naturally a fighter, his philosophy and his pugnacious instinct are constantly at war. His philosophy is stronger than his instinct, and gaining strength by exercise every day; but should the excitement of the moment ever cause him to act before his forbearance could influence him, there would be a sorry time for some one, because he is as quick on his feet as a cat, and can handle his fists like a professional prize-fighter. As for Clint, he would never bother himself to get into a fight nor trouble himself to avoid one. Sam and he are firm friends, and would make an extremely awkward couple in a street fight. This seems to be generally understood by all the people about here, and very few persons would care to provoke a quarrel with Sam the barkeeper or Butts the superintendent. Nate is a regular little angel of peace. No one can quarrel with him, and any one that would try would bring every man, woman, and child in the village about his ears. Nate is also very useful; but no matter how busy I keep him, he always finds time to visit the sick, the needy, and the unfortunate, and to share his little earnings with them. A better staff it would be impossible for me to find. Sam's advice on any subject is generally sound; he has a way of getting directly at the facts of a case. And Mr. Butts is a prodigy for carrying out and supplying mathematical details for any plan I may suggest. But when I pointed out to the last-named gentlemen a poor wretch whose necessities had compelled him to accept a position as a sneaking spy, Sam came very near forgetting his philosophy and Mr. Butts his disinclination to go out of his way for a fight. For a moment or so it was as much as Nate and I could do to prevent the two indignant men from literally wiping up my office floor with the frightened Pinkerton. After order was restored, I placed the detective in front of me, and as I did so I was surprised at what I read in his mind. Why! professor, I could see crimes enough to hang that man twenty times. As his telltale mind called up each incident of his past career, and wondered if by any possible means I could be aware of it, of course I read it, and by means of a few questions I caused the mental book to open at pages that had been sealed with blood. For a moment I was undecided what to do. I have grave doubts whether hanging a man does him or the country any good. So I only exhibited my knowledge in a few remarks that forced the criminal so-called officer of the law to turn white with fright, and beg me to say no more before witnesses. 'Sam, show the gentleman to the door,' I said; and

Sam smilingly complied, bowing with mock politeness as he opened the door for our prisoner's escape, and motioned him with a wave of his hand to leave. Not only did the detective leave, but he did so on a run, and made a bee-line for the railroad depot. There being no train, he took to the track, and the last we saw of him, he was 'counting the crossties,' as Sam expressed it, to the next town.

"And so it is with all of them. As soon as I show a knowledge of their past history, they are more than pleased to leave, with all possible speed, a section of the country where it is apparent that their real past is known or suspected. As you may imagine, it was not long before my enemies began to find great difficulty in securing detectives who were willing to watch me for evidences of insanity. After a while, when I caught a spy sneaking after me, it was only necessary to look him squarely in the face to send him scampering away like a coyote pursued by hounds.

"Everything I said or did was weighed for evidence of lack of rationality; but, what is strange, Messrs. Keene, White, and Brown will under no considerations meet me to talk over this or any other matter; they all three, I verily believe, think that I am Satan himself."

CHAPTER VII.

THE strike had come. All through the coal regions work had ceased. The great dark holes no longer diurnally swallowed up and vomited forth strings of black-faced men and boys. The tin dinner-pails ceased their chain-like clanking. Ah, the terrible silence of a strike! Ah, the hardship, privation, and suffering of a strike! Ah, the bitter disappointment, the gnawing hunger, the barren despair of a strike! Oh the cruel, cruel power of a corporation, the soulless, grinding machine which coins human blood and bone into gold!

The bleak winter wind, as it howls about the mountain, blowing the cutting, drifting snow under the doors, into the fireless

AH, THE HARDSHIP, PRIVATION AND SUFFERING OF A STRIKE!

THE LAW LOCKS UP WHAT A LOVING

rooms of the miner, is less cruel than the power that keeps mountains of fuel locked up while human beings die for lack of the genial warmth that lies latent in the unused coal. Oh, the blasphemy, the sacrilege, of the law that locks up what a loving God has created for his children!

"The people of the cities read of these strikes in their morning papers, and grumble at the inconvenience it causes them, never thinking for an instant that a strike is the last feeble effort of manhood to save itself from hopeless and degrading slavery. Why will not people use their brains, and think?" I said to the professor, who hap-

GOD HAS CREATED FOR HIS CHILDREN.

pened in the office, as he explained, to get my experiences up to date.

"Hold on, my dear fellow," answered my friend. "You must not require that of the generality of people; if you do, you are asking more than even your occult powers can accomplish. Thinking, in the true sense of the word, gives the average man the headache. I used to try to make my boys at college use their brains, and I can tell you truly, that in a class of fifty I am fortunate if I have two thinkers: the rest learn like parrots. Most men do the same. Suppose a New Yorker begins to reason upon what passes about him—what is the consequence? Perhaps the man wonders why the policeman is allowed to sneak up behind a licensed peddler near Fulton Street, in your great city of New York, and kick that peddler, one brutal kick after another, across Broadway. I saw that myself. The man thinks, and he can find no solution to the difficulty; his impulse is to ask the policeman; but he is afraid, as I was afraid, of being clubbed and sent up for ten days for 'resisting an officer.' And so the thinker asks his friend, and his friend looks at him with pity, and says, 'I hope you are not going to turn crank.'

"That frightens the ordinary man, and he ceases to think, because, as soon as he uses his brains, he finds himself separated from the crowd; he lacks confidence in himself, and argues that the crowd is right. Oh, it is much easier to take your politics from the newspaper, your science from the professors, your religion from the pulpit, than it is to study for yourself! Remember, my dear boy, it took a book on 'Moonblight,' another on magic, a fit of indigestion, and an all-night struggle before you dared see what has been before your eyes ever since you were born.

"We are gregarious; we like to be conventional, and not excite remark. What man is there among your acquaintances who dares even to eat what he likes, drink what

"THE PEOPLE IN THE CITIES READ OF THESE STRIKES AND GRUMBLE AT THE INCONVENIENCE IT CAUSES THEM."

he likes, or dress as he likes? Not one. The man who did so would be considered an idiot or desirous of creating a sensation; or, what is worse, he would be looked upon as a madman. Conservatism is a good thing as a guard against unthinking impulse; but when it stands in the way of reason; when it lumbers up our churches, filling the skin of Christianity with a stuffing of vile paganism; when it binds the shackles on the slave; when it bolsters up the tyrant and evil-doer, conservatism becomes retrogression. Just now, we are on the retrograde; but the undercurrent is gathering strength and volume for a big tidal wave of public opinion, that will come, when it does come, with an irresistible force, sweeping everything before it. I dread these tidal waves almost as much as I do conservatism. But I did not come here to lecture: I came here to learn. Pardon the interruption, and continue your story."

"Well, the strike came, and is still here," I continued; "but the Moonblight mines are working to their fullest capacity. New shafts have been opened, new breakers erected, and every improvement for facilitating work and adding to the comfort and safety of the men that Sam, Mr. Butts, or I myself could think of has been adopted. I have even purchased more coal lands adjoining those already worked. The happy faces of the men and the smiles of the poor, tired-looking women are worth more than money; and the song of the miner and the sound of his pick and shovel are music to my ears. But it is painful to see the misery of the strikers and heartrending to see the want and destitution of the strikers' families. I give employment to all the men I can, but it is impossible, even if I were to bore the hills like a rabbits' warren, to give employment to all applicants. My men deny themselves, and contribute liberally to the support of their unfortunate brothers. I have abolished the company-store system, and allow those among the miners who wish to, and are competent, to buy out the shops, and run them themselves. I divided the village up into regular lots, and leased them under ninety-nine-year leases to the highest bidders; and such was the boom business had that there was a corresponding boom in real estate. In each lease I incorporated an agreement to the effect that all the land-rent should go toward public improvements— schools and public buildings. Each leaseholder also holds a proportional part of all public buildings. Every five years a new rent-rate is to be made. In other respects it is about the same sort of document as most ninety-nine-year leases are, with the vital exception that all land-rent goes to the public, that is, back to the rent-payers again; and at my death, the village or town through their trustees inherits the property.

"Thus I have bound myself, while alive,

"HOWEVER STRONG AND MIGHTY THE BEAST MAY BE, HE CAN IN THE END BE CONQUERED BY THE DIMINUTIVE MICROBE."

and the town after my death for almost a hundred years; and I hope by that time the success of the scheme will be such that the leases will be renewed, with any improvements that experience may suggest. Sam started a building association, which, like all such associations, is a success. Look out of the window, and see the new houses going up! These men have something to live for; they see comfort and education for their little ones and rest for their old people. The sale of liquor on my property will nullify a lease. That is a bit of arbitrary power I have used; but after the reforms are permanently established, I am inclined to think it will be an unnecessary clause.

"Why do men drink? Only to procure a temporary relief from the responsibilities and cares of life. That the jollity and mirth, which should be spontaneous, can for a brief time have an artificial sway, wine is necessary at dinner. It is used as a drug to benumb care even among the wealthy or well-to-do. The solution of the temperance problem is to give a man something to work for. The solution of the religious problem is to give a man something to live for. Every man, in whatever business he may be, is practically a mine owner or a miner. We are not the only slave-drivers. Our slave system is more evident, but no more real than theirs."

"Bravo! Bravo!" cried the professor, rubbing his hands with delight.

THE EDITOR.
"OUR SLAVE SYSTEM IS MORE EVIDENT, BUT NO MORE REAL THAN THEIRS."

"The cash for the leases I receive is immediately spent upon the draining and grading of streets, the paving of sidewalks and the making of parks. Small as the village is, we already have two parks laid out. Listen a moment; hear the sounds of the saw and hammer, Professor. That is on our school-house. It will not be long before the little hamlet, that grew like a filthy fungus from the mud and mire surrounding my mines, will become a beautiful village.

"For fear that, in case of my death, the mines themselves might fall into the hands of some such diabolical combination as that which shut down the mines of *Spring Valley,

* See "A Strike of Millionaires Against Miners," by H. D. Lloyd.

ruined a happy village, starved the inhabitants, and stopped their incomes that it might foreclose the mortgages, I have caused to be recorded a grant or deed which allows the miners of Moonblight to run the mines themselves in case the owner should refuse to meet a board of arbitration that is provided for to decide any disputed point of wages. Notwithstanding all these grants, and property practically given away, my mines would still pay me large dividends were it not for Messrs. Keene, White, and Brown, and their railroad combinations."

"Well," exclaimed my companion, "I fail to see any cloud in the bright prospect before you. Your town is growing under my very eyes. That little cottage over there by the park has a roof on it now, and as I came by from the depot, there was only a patch of shingles on one side. How patriotic you are! Almost every house has a United States flag of some kind."

"Oh, yes," I replied, "that is a suggestion from Sam. He said, and rightly, that we are following out the true American principles of giving every man an equal opportunity, and that the flag stands for and is the emblem of the freedom our ancestors fought for, and does not stand for 'vested rights,' as some of our legislators would try to make us believe, any more than the teachings of Christ stand for the modern paganism of the churches. Adopting Sam's hint, I have tried to make my men, both foreign and American born, understand and believe that that flag is the symbol of the rights they have so long struggled for, and when it is used to represent anything else, it is usurpation. This helps win popular opinion and sentiment. We claim to be Americans, and declare that all oppressors, no matter what their birth may be, *are not Americans* because they do not believe in the *American principles*.

"This, professor, is the bright side, and the side I choose to look upon; but there is a shadow wherever there is a light, and in that shadow I am maligned, called a crank, a rascal, a fool, a schemer, an unprincipled speculator, and a dangerous agitator. Mr. Keene, in most scathing language, has pretended to show how I am planning to ruin all the other companies and then form a trust which will grind the laborer further into the ground than before my so-called reforms were introduced. I continue to

"TWO DISTRACTED MOTHERS WERE SOBBING OVER THE LOSS OF THEIR LITTLE ONES. ONLY GOD AND MOTHERS KNOW WHY THEY MOURNED."

ship my coal and keep the price down at the usual rates, but I must confess that Messrs. Keene, Brown and White in a measure checkmate me, by forming a railroad combination which takes all my profits in tolls.

"Gangs of foreigners began to pour in from New York—strange, greasy, dirty-looking men, many of them wearing sheepskin coats and odd-looking caps; none of them speaking English. These hordes come from the emigrant ships and are hired in gangs by the 'laborer broker.' The mining boss passes the word, 'Give me a hundred men at the same price as the last lot,' to the broker, who is a cunning fellow and squeezes a commission out of both sides for his services. By dealing in men by the wholesale, as if dealing in potatoes or corn, one is able to get wholesale prices, which are much cheaper than if the men were bought singly or in 'blocks of five,' and the employers save quite a neat sum by the process. The laborer broker goes to the gang-master, who, as soon as he receives the order, loses no time in having the potatoes—excuse me, the men—ready for delivery.

"'Huns', my miners called them, and apparently they have no other name, either personal or national; if they possess any real name it is known only to themselves and the padrones.

"Each Hun is numbered and answers to his number and is known only by that number.

"Clint told me that the padrones make a good living by securing such gangs for those who want them on short notice; and evidently the padrones are doing a flourishing business during the strikes. On pay-day the gang-master is there, and he sees to it that no Hun, be his name Mr. One or Mr. One Hundred gets more than enough to keep his poor, shivering, slavish soul inside of his greasy, poverty-stricken body. These men are to become voters. Did I say voters? No, not that; ignorant as they are, slavish as is their spirit, they are men, and could they vote, the vote would be that of freemen; but these 'Huns' will act as proxies for their different masters and cast their master's vote in numbers equal to the number of slaves on the plantation—I beg pardon—miners working in his mines.

"Things looked squally. Each car that came in brought a load of 'Huns' and loads of *guns* carried by professional cut-throats whom any one in this "Land of the Free," who has the money, can employ to shoot down their rebellious slaves. How this book of Magus plays havoc with my tongue! What I should say, so as not to offend, is—to protect his property against mobs of dissipated, whiskey-drinking men, who dare to claim the inherent right granted them by their Creator and demand the privilege of living on God's great earth, which some of them are sacrilegious enough to think was intended by their Creator for man's use and support.

"Black clouds of Huns covered the hills, and black clouds of despair shaded the brows of the poor strikers, as these foreign herds began to take their places at the mines, and eviction followed eviction, turning family after family out into the cold, bleak winter, with no shelter, no hope, and no place to go. Added to this was the galling fact of the presence of the armed guards of Pinkertons. I could not help asking myself what our ancestors would have done under such circumstances? What would Abe Lincoln have said? How would Thomas Jefferson have acted? What was *I* to do?

SPEECH ON FREE LABOR, DELIVERED SEPTEMBER, 1859.

WHAT ABE LINCOLN DID SAY.—"I hold, if the Almighty had ever made a set of men that should do all the eating and none of the work, he would have made them with mouths only, and no hands; and if he had ever made another class that he had intended should do all the work and none of the eating, he would have made them without mouths and with all hands."

"My men were kept quiet only by keeping them busy."

"Force begets force," said Professor Follium. "Peaceful methods are the only ones a Christian can use and still claim to be a Christian. A chaplain attached to a regiment is like a temperance pledge attached to a gin-mill counter. Force is the argument of the robber, the bandit, and the savage. A thief, a burglar, a desperado, is always armed, because he lives by force; takes what he gets by force, retains what he has by force, and in the end dies by force."

"Yes, professor, that is about the way Sam and I reasoned it out, when the subject of our carrying arms was broached. As for Clint, he never bothered his head about it one way or the other. Fear is a word which signified to him something that makes other people commit acts that to him are incomprehensible.

"I sent Sam among the strikers to do some stump-speaking and to advise the men to throw up the strike at once and resume their places; for I plainly saw that, with the opportunities for labor locked up under the silly laws of the country, the opportunity market is cornered; while the labor supply is practically unlimited. The strike must be a failure; and for humanity's sake I sent Sam to tell them how hopeless was their rebellion.

"Sam was the man who could do it; he could talk in a language they could understand, and use arguments that would appeal to them. But imagine my surprise and chagrin when Nate came running in one day to tell me that the Pinkertons had made a rush to capture Sam, calling him an agitator and a ringleader of rioters; that the miners had defended Sam and thrown coal and stones; that the Pinkertons had fired on the crowd and killed two boys and wounded a woman; that the crowd, being reinforced, had driven the Pinkertons back.

"Here was a situation! And as I read the newspaper accounts the next day, I was horrified to find that Sam was designated as an anarchist bar-keeper, a tough and desperate character, and that warrants were out for his arrest.

"Clint's 'fight' had come, and a serious affair it was! Two poor stiff little forms lay stretched dead in two wretched miners' huts; two distracted mothers were sobbing over the loss of their little ones. Only God and mothers know why they mourned; even my spiritual eyes could see naught before them in this life but degrading poverty, bitter want, drudgery and slavery. But none the less did two mothers sob and refuse to be comforted; two black-faced, black-handed, grizzly-headed miners ground their teeth and clenched their fists, but shed no tears—"

"All because you sent a man of peace to preach peace among them," said Professor Follium.

"No, the real reason was because the assemblage of a crowd gave the combination an opportunity to allow that gnome Force to have his way, in hope that it would create a riot and turn popular opinion on their side," I answered. "As for Sam, he was safe for the present with me, for no detective would face me. They think that I am secretly connected with their infernal bureau, and by private means keep myself posted on their misdeeds; and not one has a conscience clear enough or the courage to have his acts laid bare before witnesses. But more trouble was in store. Clint Butts was accused of leading the reinforcements that came to Sam's rescue. I sent for Clint and asked him if it was true. 'No, sir,' he replied, and I dismissed him. I then sent for

Nate to ask him about it; but he came running in, all out of breath, to tell me that Mr. Butts was in trouble—that he was attacked by a crowd of armed men. Snatching my

"FORCE BEGETS FORCE." THE DETECTIVES FAILED TO ARREST CLINT BUTTS.

hat and calling to Sam to follow, I rushed out in the direction taken by my superintendent; for I knew some one was bound to be hurt this time.

"'Here comes Buffalo Bill!' I heard shouted. 'Hurrah for Buffalo Bill of Moonblight!' cried a group of youngsters, as I dashed by, my hair flying, and Sam following close behind. We were none too soon, for, as I turned a corner of the new schoolhouse that I am having built, I saw Clint Butts standing on the scantling frame-work in front of the unfinished building, with two prostrate, bloody figures at his feet, and three more upright men staring into the muzzle of a nickel-plated revolver that glistened in the sun. It was a splendid group for a show-poster or the back of a cheap novel, and so still were they all that they might have been mistaken for wax figures, had not the steel-gray eyes of the superintendent, glinting through their fringe of long, dark lashes, moved from one to the other of the group of three.

"'Stand back, sir! They are armed!' he cried upon seeing me, but the warning was unnecessary, for Sam had noiselessly come up behind them and snatched the pistols from under the coat-tails of two of the men. He pressed a revolver against the cheek of one, and covered the second, as he quietly said:

"'Gentlemen, throw up your hands! The jack-pot is ours! It's the superintendent's next deal!' Up went six hands.

"'Clint,' I exclaimed, 'have you injured those two men?' pointing to the prostrate forms.

"'No, sir, guess not,' said Clint, with a broad smile, as he still covered the middle man, while Sam proceeded to relieve the third of his revolver. 'But Sam had better disarm this one, too,' said Clint, motioning with his foot to one recumbent figure, 'for he'll shoot as soon as he comes to.'

"Seeing no damage done, I regained my breath and composure at about the same instant, and recognized the men as being Pinkerton detectives. The blood on the two prostrate figures, I was relieved to see, came from their noses, and one look at Clint's brawny fist told the cause of the bloodshed.

"'Mr. Butts,' I said sternly, 'how came you with that pistol? I requested you not to carry arms; did I not?'

"'Yes, sir,' said Clint, still smiling; for both he and Sam appeared to think something humorous had happened. 'Yes, sir,' repeated Clint; 'but this pistol was paid for by your friend, Mr. Keene, and sent by him to me. This gentleman here,' bowing and smiling at one of the discomfited fellows at his feet, 'was kind enough to present it to me; but he awkwardly enough presented it cocked, with the muzzle aimed at my head; and had I not knocked it up with one hand while I *pushed* him away with the other, I fear you would have been minus a superintendent.'

"'Sam,' said Clint in a commanding tone, and his steel-gray eyes flashed through their black lashes, 'pile up the arsenal here! Now, you sneaks, when I say attention, stand up like men. At-ten—SHUN!' Up stood the five men. 'Right dress, eyes front!' All eyes were fixed on Clint. 'Will you step here, sir?' said Clint. I instinctively obeyed him, as the detectives had done. 'Good day, sir,' remarked the superintendent, as he handed me the shining revolver, and coolly proceeded upon his way to the mines, leaving Sam with an arsenal of weapons, and me in command of a squad of dejected-looking detectives.

"'Gentlemen,' I said, 'I will not ask you what brought you here. You know that we carry no arms, and are not accustomed to armed visitors. We are men of peace.' There seemed to be some doubt in the minds of the desperadoes about this announcement, but they discreetly said nothing. 'Sam, will you please unload these revolvers?—No, stop! This man,' said I, pointing to one of them, 'fired a pistol on August the 12th, 1872, and I do not think he will use this one here, with so many witnesses present—respectable witnesses, mind you,' I repeated, because by this time a crowd of store-keepers and workmen had collected. The man to whom I spoke turned pale, and his four companions looked curiously at him, and in their turn turned pale as I looked at them.

"'These other four gentlemen, I know, do not desire me to name their little escapades, and I will refrain from doing so. I will simply say that they will not be indiscreet in the use of their weapons ; and, as the firearms are not our property, Sam, you will kindly restore the revolvers to the owners, loaded as they are.'

"'One chamber empty in this one, sir,' said Sam sententiously.

"'The bullet is there,' said a bystander, as he pointed to a hole in the new plank just over the spot where we had seen Clint standing a few moments before.

"'Yes, that pistol went off accidentally,'

said Sam. 'The accident part was when Clint knocked der murderous weapon up wid one hand, and clipped der duffer in der nose wid der other. See? But what I don't understand,' continued the bar-keeper, unconsciously dropping his barroom slang, as I noticed he frequently did, 'is why the others did not draw their guns.'

"'They didn't have time,' said the same bystander. 'One of those men went up behind Mr. Butts, and put his hand on Mr. Butts's shoulder, and was just about to say something to him when all of a sudden he dropped, and Mr. Butts was facing them all. The other man pulled out that big revolver, and it went off almost as soon as he got it out; but before I could see how 'twas done, Mr. Butts had the revolver, and the man was down alongside the first one. The other three had their hands under their coat-tails. Then Sam came running over, and you know the rest.'

"'Gentlemen,' I continued after the interruption, 'here is your property. Take it and leave, and you will confer a great favor on me, the next time you have business to transact or legal papers to present, if you will leave your arms at headquarters, and not present your pistol before presenting the paper. As your paper does not concern me, I will bid you good day.'

"Had it not been for Sam and Nate, the crowd would have jeered the discomfited 'Slinkertons,' as Sam styles them. Some of the small boys did hurrah for Buffalo Bill, a name irreverently bestowed upon me on account of my flowing locks. The Pinkertons left, as I knew they would, to tell their comrades stories of the long-haired detective that 'was onto them all,' and to wonder who the individual could be who looked like a cowboy and played the mine owner's part. These men had a warrant for the arrest of Clint Butts, but they did not show it or mention it; in fact, never a word did they utter, but, taking their arms, marched off, not as if they had been whipped, but with the air of men who had misunderstood orders, and, through no fault of their own, had got into some trouble as a consequence. They were evidently glad enough to get away from me; for my fame was now firmly established among them as the king of detectives."

CHAPTER VIII.

THE next day I showed the professor all the new buildings, the new school-house, the parks, and the mines; and Sam and Mr. Butts were delighted with an opportunity to explain all the details of their work to a man who not only could understand their explanations and the difficulties overcome, but could appreciate their success, whether it was shown in a building, a mine, or the formation of a circulating library.

When we returned to the office, and the professor's pipe was lighted, he announced it as his opinion that I had been going through some incantation; "For," said he, "nothing but magic could produce such results in so short a time."

"Magic it is, professor," said Sam; "and it's real old Yankee-doodle American magic, too."

"Yes, sir," said Clint. "My employer is truly a magician."

"Clint," said I, "I thought you were too practical to stoop to a compliment, and too much of a materialist to use such a term, even in joke."

"The real materialist," interrupted the professor, "is unconsciously spiritual; every experiment of his, every bit of knowledge he acquires, every truth or partial truth he discovers, aids the vision of the spiritual eyes of such as use them. I take a walk with you by the sea-shore; the old ocean rolls in, in, in, one roll after another thundering on the beach; the blue sky overhead is reflected in the mirror of water below, but, on account of the unevenness of the waves, the sea is a deeper, darker blue than the sky overhead; the distant sails look like flecks of white on the horizon, the sea-birds like snow-flakes. This much we see together, this much we enjoy together; but here it ends. What to me are only sails on the horizon, to your nautical eyes are schooners, coasters, yachts, and pilot-boats; what to me is only a dark-blue sea, to your yachtsman's eyes is a stiff sailing breeze; what to you is only a sandy beach is to me the wrecks of continents, ground to atoms, and the atoms polished like gems by the ceaseless grinding of Old Neptune's mill; what to you is a bit of shell, to me is a valuable and heretofore mislaid page in Nature's volume of Conchology; what to both of us is sky and water, to an artist would be a scheme of color. In other words, we each 'have eyes and we see not,' because we see only what our eyes are educated to see, or what we look for. You point out to me the peculiarities of form of a distant sail, and I notice them for the first time. You explain to me that such a rig is carried only by a certain style of craft, and the next time I see that peculiar cut of sail, I know what sort of craft it is off on the horizon. So I learn that those dark spots on the water are squalls, and my nautical eyes are partly opened. In my turn, I explain the action of the sea in wearing away the shores in some places by undermining the cliffs and causing them to cave into the water; then, by using the fragments to grind against each other, and the waves as motive power, with time unlimited, I show you how the pieces are ground to small fragments called sand, and the next time you visit the beach you examine a handful of sand, and your only partially opened eyes will detect the different rocks and the quartz which originally composed the cliffs or shores of some unchronicled land. So the materialist unconsciously aids the vision of the man he despises as a dreamer. So you, my friend, have partly opened my spiritual eyes, and even though I see things but dimly through the green glasses of science, still the green glass, by giving a oneness of color to all objects, suggests to me what may possibly be a truth to you; that is, that there is no such distinction as natural and spiritual laws. Either they are all spiritual or all natural; and furthermore, there can be but one Church, and that is the brotherhood of man; and but one dogma in that Church, and that is love—by love meaning the sentiment which prompts us to worship God by working for the welfare of others, to seek to benefit and give pleasure to others, and to derive our own pleasure from so doing. But these things that appear so plain to you and me, are only words to a third party; the fleck of white is only a sail to him, the beach is only sand. His eyes are closed, and will not open."

"Ah, no, professor; there you err. He of whom you speak is the baser metal, and to turn him into pure gold you must have the *prima materia* which the pigskin-covered book tells us is to be found in yourself: 'Every one has it, from the beggar to the king.' I have searched for that *lapis philosophorum*, and found it. So have you, but you were unconscious of it. It is love. With love you can make the blind see; love will transmute the baser metals into pure gold, but there will be only as much pure gold as there is 'essence of gold' in the baser metal. I agree with you in most things. You have aided my sight most wonderfully, and unless that sight betrays me, there is but one thing taught from the beginning to the end of the gospel, and that is love. You expressed it in your talk on use. A useful man is the only religious man. All idlers are pagans, whether they wear the garb of the Church, the millionaire, or the tramp."

"Thet's der kind of magic that's built this place, professor, and nary a blamed preacher, barring my boss and myself, in der town," said Sam.

"What's the matter with me?" said Clint.

"Well, professor, Mr. Butts is one of der silent-preacher kind; he don't talk much wid his mouth, but he's great on a prayer, you bet! Oh, he's a one-er when it comes to praying!" Sam announced enthusiastically.

"Why, Sam, you wretch! I have not said my prayers since I was a lad."

"Have n't, eh?" replied the bar-keeper. "Why, you're at it all der time. You pray thet a hole shall be made in der mountain, and you pray wid pick, shovel, gunpowder, and surveying implements. And, gewhillikens! Lo! there's der hole. Prayer answered; see? Now, take all those make-believe Christians thet pray for der poor people on Sundays, and work all der week to make them poorer, what is their real prayer? They get down on their marrow-bones to try to fool der Good Lord on Sunday, and pray all der week by their work just der other way. What a man works for, he is praying for; see? What he says wid his mouth don't amount to nothing; thet ain't his prayer. In a whole churchful of people, how many are game enough to put der real prayer in words, so thet all could hear? 'Bout one, I reckon, in a hundred."

"Come, Sam, don't be too hard on the

church people, for I intend to build a big church, and make you a deacon; and all preachers that choose to come here shall be allowed to preach from the pulpit of that church, and say just what suits them. But no one denomination shall ever have control. They are all brothers, or they are not Christians."

"Geewhiz! Let der bug hop, sir! I'm in for thet church!" said Sam, as we all parted for the night.

Again I bade farewell to my genial friend, the professor; the only one of my former friends that I have seen since leaving my yacht, months ago, at Port Jefferson, L. I. A feeling of sadness crept over me, as I saw my learned ally board the train to continue his lecturing tour—a feeling of loneliness that I could not dispel. Moonblight, in spite of the snow, in spite of the frost, was flourishing. Sleighbells jingled in the streets, the merry voices of children could be heard on the hillsides, as their heavily loaded sleds spun down the icy slopes. The American flag floated from the liberty-pole in the park, and the smoke that came from the cottage chimneys told that there were warm fires within; but I was alone: the pleasant greetings I received from each passer-by somehow failed to cheer me, as I tramped back through the snow. The desolate specter of the strike seemed to leer like some monster over the mountains, and with hungry eyes to threaten the peace and prosperity of our little village. I knew that if the coal companies could by any means crush my town they would do so, and that the laws of the State, if they did not uphold them, would never help me. I should be crushed, law or no law.

The air was crisp and cold, the snow under foot squeaked and crunched, plainly indicating that every drop of moisture in it was transformed into brilliant crystals, and, as a gust of wind would blow up a little cloud of snow, and twist it around in a miniature whirlwind, the icy particles glistened in the sun like a shower of diamonds. Christmas greens decorated the shops, but the dark clouds of doubt and helplessness so filled my mind that the invigorating air, the merry voices, and the Christmas greens were unable to dispel them. I reached my office-door, turned the knob, and entered.

Throwing myself into an office-chair in front of the dying embers of the fire, I did nothing to repel the attack of melancholy

THE OLD PATHS.

which already had possession of me; but, on the contrary, I threw open the gates of my mind and heart, spiked the guns of hope, and banished all cheerful thoughts.

Not only did I not repel the enemy, but I gave it a hearty welcome, and, as thousands of people are doing at this very moment, I coddled and warmed the invading "blue devils" in my bosom into stronger life—fed them on morbid thoughts until they grew fat.

I abandoned myself to the luxury of being perfectly miserable.

What is the use of trying to do right? Why make an attempt to do anything differently from other men?

The old paths are the safest to travel; they are well worn, free from underbrush and briers, and supplied with a goodly company of jolly traveling companions.

New paths are guarded by unknown monsters; the ground, strewn with sharp stones, is full of pitfalls; thorns and briers impede the way, but fail to hide the bleaching bones and grinning skulls of former explorers.

Why not return to my old, careless life in New York City?

Why? Because it is too late—too late. I

have passed that stage of my life's journey, I thought, and it would be as impossible for me to return to it as it would be to go back to my twenty-first birthday.

I imagine the utter dreariness of gazing, day after day, from the club window on Fifth Avenue, only varying the monotony by an

A RED-FACED OLD CLUBMAN.

occasional Manhattan cocktail; to sit and dawdle with my glass and cigar, and watch the toiling mass of humanity that pass the club windows, and to know that one and all, the typewriter, the stage-driver, the clerk, the fruit-vender and the scavenger, are all toiling to supply me with a club window, cocktails and the companionship of some red-faced, gray-haired old clubmen, or loose-jointed, big, flabby, white-faced young clubmen.

No, it is too late; and the company of the frost-headed old idlers would drive me from the club-rooms, while the sight of the helplessly inane faces of the younger men would cause me to wish that I had never been born.

Better to fight my fight at Moonblight; but, oh, how lonesome I felt! I had developed great affection for Sam and Clint, but they were not the boon companions to whom I had been so long accustomed. Oh! for some one to whom to go when I felt tired; some one to help me with an encouraging word or suggestion; some one to—

The office door flew open, a gust of bitter cold air and Sam rushed in. Sam's dark eyes were snapping, as he exclaimed:

"Well, sir, there is the devil to pay, and no mistake!"

I motioned him to take a seat, which he did, first helping himself to an armful of small sticks from the wood-box, casting them on the embers in the wide-gaping fireplace.

"Well?" I said.

"'T ain't well at all, sir!" and Sam gave

the fire a vicious punch with a small crowbar we used for a poker. "Them Hessians—dod rat their ornery hides!—" and the barkeeper banged the wood such a blow that the sparks went flying up the chimney.

"Well, the Hessians, Sam, who are they?"

"Oh, those Slinkerton detectives who have been prowling around with der guns as if dey were wid Stanley in Africa! Well, one of them's got a head as red as a Japanese devil; and Big Buck Thornton, he laughed at him, called him Carrot Top, and asked him if he was laying around looking for white horses. With that all the strikers by the breaker laughed, and it made the Slinkerton so mad that he up with his Winchester and fired into the crowd, and killed—"

"Whom?" I exclaimed.

"Another woman, of course!" said the barkeeper. "The strikers," he continued, "are gathering in force, and swear revenge. All our men want to aid the strikers, and it is as much as Clint and I can do to keep the mines working. Our men say blood is thicker than water; the strikers are their brothers, and our miners argue that to keep quiet while a band of hired ruffians shoot down their neighbors' wives and children is simply cowardice. Clint and I have put on extra gangs of men wherever we could find room for them, and we are doin' our best to keep all hands so busy that they will not have time to get in harm's way. But there's going to be trouble over there"; and Sam scowled at the mountains that separated our village and mines from those of my enemies and former associates.

So my gloomy forebodings were not without cause. However odd it may appear, now that trouble was in sight I felt a strange reaction and a certain gay buoyancy of spirit as I listened to Sam's narrative. As the real trouble approached, the gloomy forebodings fled.

A week passed, and the subdued grumblings of the strikers could be heard everywhere. A mass-meeting was held, and the Pinkertons denounced as murderers. This incendiary language being reported, the sheriff demanded assistance, and the governor of the commonwealth ordered out the militia: they were even now expected, Sam informed me. The words had barely escaped his lips when I heard the drums, and, to my horror, they sounded as if they were marching through Moonblight. Next, I heard hooting and shouting.

Snatching my hat, I rushed out, to behold, marching up toward the main street of the village, a regiment of our State Guards, surrounded on all sides by a mob of women and children.

As I approached nearer, I could could see that most of the soldiers were young fellows with smooth faces; but among the officers were a few grizzled men, upon whose breasts hung the bronze star worn by veterans of the late civil war. Hastening up to one of them, whose shoulder-straps proclaimed him to be the colonel, I touched my hat, and, walking by his horse's side, asked him if he could not march his regiment by some other route, calling his attention to the wild, half-scared looks with which his boyish soldiers viewed the screaming mob. I told him that I feared some accident would cause an outbreak in my peaceful town.

The colonel was courteous, as are all veterans, and replied that his judgment agreed with mine, but that he had positive orders to move his men as he did. My enemies had political influence, and were using it, it was evident, to tempt my men to riot.

NEW PATHS.
THORNS AND BRIERS IMPEDE THE WAY, BUT FAIL
TO HIDE THE BLEACHING BONES AND GRINNING
SKULLS OF FORMER EXPLORERS.

A piece of ice came whizzing by the colonel and me; and as we turned, in alarm, another piece struck the color-sergeant, and he fell forward. It was the work of some boys, and I rushed into the crowd to stop them. A gang of miners, with their pails in hand, were just above us on the path, watching the parade. I had only time to notice this when I heard a shot, another, then an irregular volley, followed by screams and curses. I saw the old colonel, sword in hand, shouting to his men; I saw the miners rushing toward us; then I felt a sudden blow in my side, and, turning around to see who had struck me, I was astonished to find myself alone. When I removed my hand from the spot where I had felt the blow, it was covered with blood! I was shot!

Yet at first I felt no inconvenience, except a numb sensation where the bullet entered.

Meantime, the riot was at its height. I saw one woman pull off her stocking: there was blood on it; but there was more on it before the day was over; for, slipping a round lump of coal in the foot, and tying a knot in the leg of the stocking, she used her hose as a war-club with terrible effect upon the heads of the soldiers.

The worst had come. I knew not what to do. My shouts were unheeded. I was surrounded by demons—not human beings. Every eye was staring, each hand grasped whatsoever weapon came handy, and with only one purpose—to kill. Another shout, and a band of detectives came dashing down the street with their Winchesters. The broken ranks of the State troops reunited.

I saw the little humpbacked figure of Nate bending over a wounded woman. I saw a burly detective level his revolver and fire, and the lad drop. The next instant a square-faced man, with heavy, bull-dog jaws and a black mustache, appeared. Although apparently unarmed, he walked slowly up to the detective, without any show of excitement. I shouted, but my voice was weak, and I could not rise from the sitting posture I had unconsciously assumed.

The detective evidently was under the impression that the man meant to surrender; but the impression was of short duration. I heard Clint's familiar voice say, "Take that, you cowardly Hessian!" And the representative of private enterprise and the lack of law doubled up from an unexpected blow in the abdomen, only to receive an upper cut in the face.

"Down with the Hessians!" cried another voice; and Sam, the bar-keeper, ran to Clint's side.

My head swam; but, with an almost superhuman effort I gained my feet and staggered toward my men.

"Colonel!" I shouted, "Colonel! for God's sake, stop the firing! They are killing innocent people!"

At last I was noticed, and my men became quiet. The colonel got control of his regiment, but the detectives had not yet played their part; for they meant that there should be a riot at Moonblight, and they had no intention of allowing it to subside until it had reached an important magnitude. Riots are their stock in trade; without them their calling is gone, and here was an opportunity not to be missed. At the same time, they had a number of old scores of a personal nature to settle with both Clint and Sam, and no sooner were my aids recognized by the detectives than a grand rush was made to capture them as "ringleaders."

The bar-keeper and the superintendent were standing side by side, alone, and only a short distance ahead of me.

"Fire one shot, move one step, and we will

THE WOMAN'S WAR-CLUB.

blow the whole durned lot of you to hell!" shouted Sam; and I saw the two friends each take a couple of oblong packages from their pockets.

"Dynamite! Clint! Sam!" I cried; then reeled. The troops and the rioters ran in circles around me; the earth heaved, and struck my face—I saw no more.

* * * * * * *

The grizzled old colonel sat with Sam and Clint on the ground, and, with the aid of the colonel's sword, they cut up a detective into square pieces. Clint used these to build a wall with; it took the united strength of the three to lift some of the stones in place. I was deeply interested in the operation, when one of them turned to look at me. It was not the colonel, Sam, nor Clint, it was Mr. Keene, in immaculate collar and cuffs.

He and his associates placed the pieces of flesh—it was Humpy's flesh—into the letter-press, and squeezed out, not blood, but gold, which they divided amongst themselves. How they watched each other! How disgraceful! Without exception, each, as opportunity offered, helped himself from his neighbor's pile.

I was mistaken; for, after all, it was only a group of chickens eating corn in the back yard of the old farm in Ohio. Oh, no; I was not in the least alarmed, for how could the old rooster reach me, and I safe in the second story and the window down?

But, horror! the old cock's neck began to stretch; it grew longer and longer; the head reached the window, and the great, blazing eye peered in at me. Grandmother came into the room just in time, and the neck receded and the head disappeared.

If Grandmother would only come to my bedside, and smooth my pillow, instead of standing at the opposite end of the room, and reaching her long arms across the bed-chamber, I would not be afraid of her.

Professor Follium came in, and, breaking open two dynamite cartridges, he poured the contents into the binnacle light, took out his watch, looked at it, then examined the mining-pumps I had in my wrist. I told him that one needed a new valve, and he, saying that Clint would attend to that, asked me to have a drink with him. I called the steward, and he brought us two glasses of wine. Then the professor examined the pumps, and again looked at his watch, smiled, left the cockpit, and disappeared over the stern. The wine had a soothing effect, and I think I must have fallen asleep and slept soundly until I was conscious of a faint perfume greeting my nostrils—a perfume so faint that I was not sure it did not emanate from my imagination; yet it was a strangely familiar perfume. It took me back to the city, to the theatre, to the ball-room, to a certain particular ball-room, and I remembered the hostess and all the guests.

I remembered, and I felt a blush crimson my face as memory brought up the conservatory, the tropical plants, the rare flowers, the strange caged birds. But it was not the plants, the flowers, or the birds that made me blush: it was the sight of a girlish face, a slight, girlish figure, and two lustrous dark eyes that looked timidly into mine as the hostess presented me.

This was the girl I was too cowardly to see; this was the girl whose true heart had never doubted mine through all my unaccountable absence; and I felt the warm blood suffuse my face again for shame that I could ever have been afraid to see her as she really was.

The perfume grew more apparent. I imagined that I felt a soft, caressing hand stroke my hair. I was dreaming, for I heard my name repeated twice. It was a pleasant dream, and, looking up, I beheld those same lustrous eyes, the same timid look, the same girlish face; and then the voice said:

"Do you know me, dear? There—don't speak!" And a slender white finger was placed upon my lips. The delirium was over, and I was making my long-postponed visit at her house.

THE END.

SIX FEET OF ROMANCE.

SIX FEET OF ROMANCE.

SOMETHING unaccountable had happened. A hand, a real, *live hand*, in a long lace mitten that allowed the tapering white fingers with their pink tips to show, reached out of the surrounding haze.

To say that I was astonished is to describe in very mild terms the dazed state in which I sat and stared. Left alone in my studio, I had been examining some new treasure-trove in the shape of small household articles, mementos of the home life of the last century, which it had been my good fortune to rescue from junk and attic rubbish.

Thanks are due the Cosmopolitan Publishing Company for kind permission to reprint, from their magazine, the illustrations which accompany this story.

From my earliest boyhood ancient wearing apparel, old household and kitchen utensils, and antique furniture have appealed to me with peculiar force; telling facts, and relating incidents in such a plain, homely, but graphic manner of the every-day life of our ancestors, that I look upon them more as text-books than as curiosities; for it is only by the light of truth, reflected from these objects, that we are enabled to brush away the romance that tinges the most ordinary facts, or pierce the rose-hued atmosphere of fiction with which the perspective of years surrounds the commonest objects of those remote times.

My antique frying-pans, toasters, and waffle-irons all have very long handles; the andirons of the same date rear their massive brass heads several feet above their strong wrought-iron cross-bars.

How plainly these things tell us of the great log fires that roared in their ample fire-places, in the brave old days of our great-grandsires! How the reflected flames must have glistened in the polished brass knobs on the andirons, and cast a warm glow on the powdered wigs of courtly dames, sparkled on the hilts of young gallants' swords, and flushed the pretty faces of maids in their finery of stiff pointed waists and rich flowered brocades!

I had been gazing especially with a gratified, satisfied sense of ownership at what I considered the gem of my find—an old-fashioned foot-stove.

This is not the ordinary tin box, such as one finds among the carefully preserved relics of any well-cared-for colonial homestead. It is a foot-stove of more than ordinary beauty of form and make. The square box that forms the stove proper is of iron, hammered by hand into thin sheets, the top and sides of which are perforated with small holes arranged in complicated and intricate designs, while the

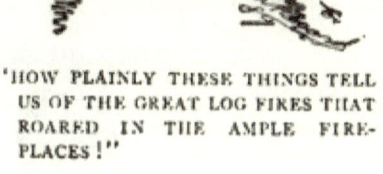

"HOW PLAINLY THESE THINGS TELL US OF THE GREAT LOG FIRES THAT ROARED IN THE AMPLE FIRE-PLACES!"

framework which holds the box is made of quaintly carved mahogany. The door forms one side of the stove, and it stood open, showing within the metal cup that still held the ashes of coals which had glowed and burned over a hundred years ago. I ob-

"THE DOOR FORMS ONE SIDE OF THE STOVE, AND IT STOOD OPEN, SHOWING WITHIN THE METAL CUP."

served the top crosspieces of the wooden frame were worn in their middle to thin strips by the generations of feet that had warmed their toes over the hot embers.

You know when you look continuously and intently at one object for a long time, all your surroundings will become misty, indistinct, and finally disappear. That was the way with the old foot-stove, as I gazed at it.

Down a hundred feet or more below me, Broadway's rumbling, bustling tide was beginning to ebb. The orange-colored gas-jets had commenced to glimmer, and the purplish glare of the fierce electric lights made sputtering nebulæ in the misty rain. But of this I seemed to be aware through an interior sense, for all my powers of physical sight were occupied in watching a most wonderful occurrence—a hand had reached out of the haze surrounding my foot-stove, and taken the metal cup from the open door, and vanished.

I can scarcely expect my readers to believe this, and I hardly believed the evidence of my own eyes—but there was my foot-stove empty. A circular mark in the dust covering the rusty iron floor of the stove alone bore witness of the recent presence of the metal cup.

I sat and stared blankly until aroused by the presence of the same beautiful, delicate, feminine hand, which replaced the iron cup in the stove, closed and latched the door, and melted away. Thin threads of blue smoke streamed through the perforations of the iron

box, like incense, and I was conscious of the odor of burning wood that awakened memories of an old Kentucky log-house, familiar to my boyhood; but the house was forgotten

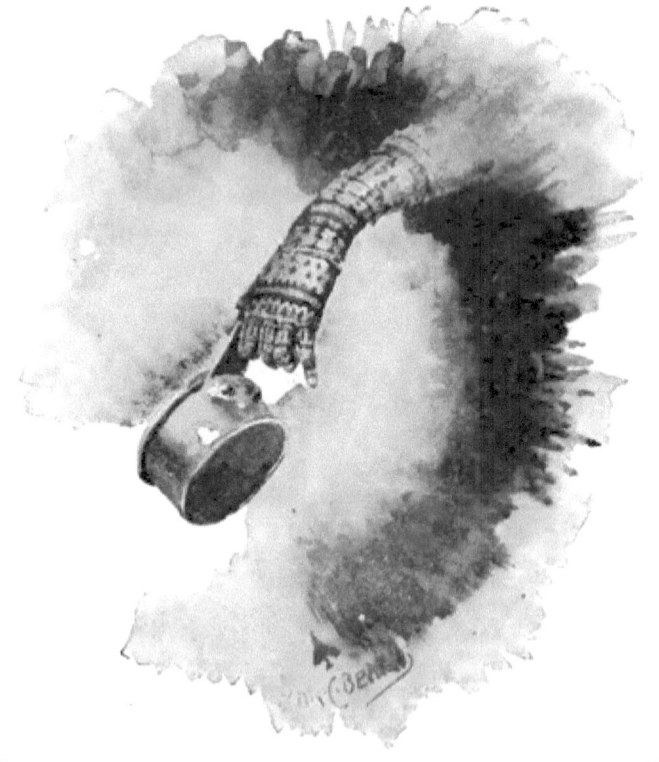

"A HAND HAD REACHED OUT OF THE HAZE SURROUNDING MY FOOT-STOVE AND TAKEN THE METAL CUP."

when I saw, materialized from the cloudy haze, a foot—oh, such a dainty foot!

The quaint, red silken shoe that incased this new visitor was latched over the instep with a silver buckle, and the shoe had the highest of high heels. The slender ankle, with its silken hose, that faded away in the surrounding mists, or was modestly hidden by the filmy lace of an overhanging skirt, was as delicate as the fairy foot in its quaintly shaped shoe, that now rested on the top of the well-worn crosspiece of the ancient foot-warmer.

There were two feet, as I could plainly see, side by side, absorbing the genial heat that filtered through the perforations from the glowing coals inside the box, but they apparently remained only a sufficient time to assure their owner that the coals inside were warm and bright: then they were gone, and I heard, or thought I heard, the rustling of a stiff gown and skirts.

The hand was now again visible, this time covered with a red woolen mitten, and grasping the handle of my foot-stove it lifted it from the floor and moved off.

But all these unaccountable and wonderful occurrences were not sufficiently startling to blind me to the fact that my much-prized antique was about to be taken away from me. It was not my desire to break the continuity of such wonderful occurrences by any rash act; but the loss of my treasure was not to be contemplated, and even the knowledge that it was in the possession of such fascinating hands and feet did not prevent me from hastily rising to follow it.

"THERE WERE TWO FEET, AS I COULD PLAINLY SEE, SIDE BY SIDE."

My memory fails to recall how it was we reached the ground, without descending the long flight of stairs in the building. However, I was presently conscious of walking over uneven and unfamiliar pavements, totally different from Broadway.

Right in front and but a short distance ahead of me tripped the red silken shoes, their high wooden heels tinkling over the frozen ground. Presently my attention was arrested and my wonder increased by meeting a pair of yellow-topped boots, that I at once recognized as a pair that I had left hanging, along with some buckskin trousers, upon my studio wall. I knew them at a glance, and their identification was complete, when I saw the new heels which I had had put on them, and the tear in the top of one, made by the struggles of a fat model in his frantic efforts to pull the boot-leg over his bulky calf. (The leather in these ancient foot-coverings is so dry and brittle that unless great care is taken, it will tear like paper.)

I have always regarded these old boots with a feeling akin to awe, imagining that they must have been worn by some powdered and buckled hero, like the "old-fashioned Colonel," who "galloped through the white infernal powder cloud," but if they had been upon the feet of a country bumpkin, they could scarcely have appeared to worse advantage than they did as they hesitated and halted beside the little red shoes. With toes turned in, the boots shuffled uneasily about, almost tripping over each other in their embarrassment.

There is a witchery about a beautiful woman that envelops her like a mantle, reaching and covering even her feet. It is,

"MY WONDER WAS INCREASED BY MEETING A PAIR OF YELLOW-TOPPED BOOTS."

in fact, as if she were surrounded by a peculiar atmosphere, which not only obscures or hides all defects of mind or body, but at the same instant brings into greater prominence all her exquisite loveliness.

It was probably a perception of this that made the boots so self-conscious. As for the high-heeled shoes, they behaved in a most coquettish manner, which apparently only tended to heighten rather than impair their charm.

However that may be, the rarest old costume in America could not have tempted me to stand in those old boots.

The greeting over, the two pairs moved off together, and I followed after them, having now a double interest—a pair of boots and a foot-stove. True, the boots are old and worn; one is a duplicate of the other, or, as a shoemaker would say, they are not "rights and lefts." The toes are bluntly pointed and stiff, but I know of no other boots of the same make and date, and that is the reason they are dear to me.

They did not appear to be in the least dear to those little reckless feet in the red, buckled shoes, and I made a mental note, as they tripped carelessly on, how the high heels prevented the small feet from touching aught but their toes to the earth, while the great broad-soled, pointed-toed, square-heeled boots moved along humbly and awkwardly, slap! slap! slap! beside their tiny companions.

The amount of emotion and thought that can be expressed by feet was a revelation to me. Such graphic expression of, not only character, but incident and feeling as well, gave an additional interest to this strange adventure, and the interest grew to excitement when I saw a pair of Wellington boots

"I HAVE ALWAYS REGARDED THESE OLD BOOTS WITH A FEELING AKIN TO AWE."

come walking briskly up. I knew them, knew them well, for I had often tried to induce their owner to part with them. They belonged to a studio in the Sherwood Building. As the new-comers came in sight, my boots looked mad. One would think it impossible for a pair of boots to show anger, but the manner in which my old Continentals set themselves squarely upon the ground, the bluntly pointed toes turned out in a dignified yet defiant manner, was very expressive, and as unmistakable as a clenched fist or a corrugated brow.

A moment's hesitation, and the little red shoes ran ahead to meet the Wellingtons, and there they stood, side by side, the newcomers a great deal closer to the dainty silken toes than my poor boots had dared to come. Intuitively I began to take sides with my property; my sympathies were all with the Continentals, and I was aware of an undignified prejudice and jealousy toward an old pair of Wellington boots.

As the pedestrians started on their walk again, the feminine shoes guarded by the Continentals and Wellingtons on either side, I followed, fully determined to pursue the adventure to an end.

The foot-path that we traveled was strewn with dead leaves and edged with grass. No thought of where we were disturbed me, but I was impressed with the feeling that the Wellington boots were trying to monopolize the attention of the red shoes, and either ignoring my Continentals entirely, or acknowledging their presence only by slighting or flippant remarks; and my surmises were in a measure confirmed by the occasional grinding twist of a Continental heel into the frozen sod.

Presently we turned into a well-traveled road, where there seemed to be many feet,

"IT WAS PROBABLY A PERCEPTION OF THIS THAT MADE THE BOOTS SO SELF-CONSCIOUS."

all walking in the same direction. Their destination proved to be a building, which we entered after ascending some wooden steps. A musty odor, peculiar to hymn-books and woodwork which only receive an airing once a week, proclaimed the building to be a church.

If it was cold inside the edifice I was not

reminded of it until the little red-mittened hand placed the old foot-stove near by, and the same fascinating red-clothed feet hopped upon it. Close upon one side were my old Continental boots, and upon the other side the Wellingtons.

It was with ill-concealed impatience that I watched the egotistical wrinkles assumed by the impertinent, uptown studio boots, and I felt my blood tingle with anger when they rested their varnished and polished toes against my old foot-stove, upon the top of which the little red shoes were perched.

For a time all three pairs of foot-gear maintained a deportment sufficiently discreet for church manners, but the way the Continentals finally kicked over a wooden footstool satisfied me that they at least were not in a receptive mood for the sermon.

Although conscious, in a general way, of my surroundings, my senses of hearing and of sight were focused upon the three pairs of feet, and what did not immediately affect them made no impression upon me.

I suppose the benediction was said, but I heard neither sermon, hymn, nor benediction, and only judged the services had ended by the movement of the feet.

When the dainty, high-heeled shoes had descended from their perch upon the foot-warmer, two hands reached down simultaneously, as if to take the stove. One was

"TWO HANDS REACHED DOWN SIMULTANEOUSLY AS IF TO TAKE THE STOVE."

broad, muscular and sunburned; the other was gloved, but showed an aristocratic narrowness and length of fingers, and, notwithstanding the rich lace frill which fell partly over it from the wrist, there was nothing weak or effeminate in its appearance.

While I could not help admiring the refinement and genteel proportions of the gloved hand, I disliked it all the more for its good points. There was a momentary struggle between those two hands for the possession of my foot-stove, but it was soon evident that the brown fingers had been too quick for their rivals, and the latter retired, only to immediately reappear with a small visiting card between the index and the second fingers.

Once again we were walking over the frozen ground of the country road, retracing our steps, and we had proceeded quite a distance, when my strange guides stopped for a moment, and then departed. The red shoes tripped lightly away until they passed the base of two large stone posts, but walked more slowly as they continued up a well-kept path.

To my surprise, the boots did not offer to follow, but both pairs strode briskly together off in an opposite direction.

Here was a dilemma I had not anticipated. I was morally certain the red shoes had carried off my foot-stove, but when I thought of my Continentals disappearing in company with those Wellingtons I decided to follow the boots, consoling myself with the thought that the stove was probably safe, and that, in the ordinary and natural course of events, the boots would be sure to find the silken shoes again, and I my foot-warmer.

We left the road, and walked Indian file through underbrush and briers to what ap-

"ONLY TO IMMEDIATELY REAPPEAR WITH A SMALL VISITING CARD BETWEEN THE INDEX AND SECOND FINGERS."

peared to be a clearing in the woods. I was glad to be out of the brambles; for, knowing the fragile condition of my old boots, I greatly feared there would be nothing left of the top leather, and so interested was I in looking them over to count the damage, that I at first failed to notice their odd pose. With toes pointing at right angles from each other, the boots stood planted wide apart, with a peculiar, and I thought somewhat dangerous, look, if such a term may be used, when my attention was attracted by a clink and ring of metal, and, raising my eyes, I saw two gleaming steel blades — two long, bright swords fencing in midair, lunging and parrying away in fine style.

My heart fairly stood still with excitement. I dreaded lest some lunge or stab might bring a pale, intense face within the circle of my vision.

It was skillful and brave work. That broad, brown hand was as firm as iron, yet as supple in the wrist as a steel spring; and its long, thin, white-lace-edged antagonist was as quick and vicious as a cat's paw.

For an instant the only movement of the crossed swords was a nervous tremor, then, like a flash, came a quick stroke and a twist. Up went one sword with a ringing sound, glinting into the air.

Bravo! I was about to cry, when I was hushed by the appearance of that same soft, feminine, lace-mittened hand, much whiter now than before. It grasped the victorious blade and closed the pretty fingers tightly over the wicked, shining steel, while its trembling mate rested upon the big, broad, brown hand that still held the sword on guard. There was a moment's pause; then the sword dropped, and two brown, sinewy hands grasped the little, mittened fingers in a rapturous, uncontrollable sort of way, which not only plainly said that they cared not to press their vantage with the sword, but that they would brave anything for the sake of holding those little lace-mittened fingers.

To make sure to whom the brown hands belonged, I cast down my eyes, and saw, as I felt I would, my old Continental boots. They were now no longer awkward, but with a sturdy, manly, happy stride, they walked alongside the red, silken, high-heeled, buckled shoes, and while these looked just as pretty, just as dainty and just as piquant as ever, they had not now any suggestion of coquetry about them.

As they moved off I followed, until we came suddenly upon my old foot-stove, where it had been hastily dropped by the side of the path. While I looked at it, the boots and shoes passed on. I noticed that the stove-door was open, and all looked dark within.

The haze around the old foot-warmer gradually melted away, and I saw reflections of the lights from the streets dancing upon the walls of my studio, and in the dusky shadows I could trace what appeared to be my old Continental boots hanging alongside the buckskin trousers.

I jumped from my seat, lighted a match, and examined the old foot-stove. The cinders were still in the metal cup. I moistened my finger with my tongue, touched the cinders, but they were *cold!*

Standard Publications

ISSUED BY

Chas. L. Webster & Co.

67 FIFTH AVE., NEW YORK.

MARK TWAIN'S BOOKS.

Adventures of Huckleberry Finn.—Holiday edition. Square 8vo, 366 pages. Illustrated by E. W. Kemble. Sheep, $3.25; cloth, $2.75.

New Cheap Edition of Huckleberry Finn.—12mo, 318 pages, with a few illustrations. Cloth, $1.00.

The Prince and the Pauper.—A square 8vo volume of 411 pages. Beautifully illustrated. Sheep, $3.75; cloth, $3.00.

A Connecticut Yankee in King Arthur's Court.—A square 8vo of 575 pages; 221 illustrations by Dan Beard. Half morocco, $5.00; sheep, $4.00; cloth, $3.00.

Mark Twain Holiday Set.—Three volumes in a box, consisting of the best editions of "Huckleberry Finn," "Prince and Pauper," and "A Connecticut Yankee." Square 8vo. Uniform in size, binding, and color. Sold only in sets. Cloth, $6.00.

Merry Tales.—In *Fiction, Fact, and Fancy Series*. This volume contains some of Mark Twain's most entertaining sketches. Among them are his personal reminiscences of the war in "The Private History of a Campaign that Failed;" a short story entitled "Luck," and his popular farce, "Meisterschaft." 12mo, 210 pages. Stamped cloth, gilt titles, 75 cents.

Standard Publications of C. L. Webster & Co.

Mark Twain's "Library of Humor."—A volume of 145 Characteristic Selections from the Best Writers, together with a Short Biographical Sketch of Each Author quoted. Compiled by Mark Twain. Nearly 200 illustrations by E. W. Kemble. 8vo, 707 pages. Full Turkey morocco, $7.00; half morocco, $5.00; half seal, $4.25; sheep, $4.00; cloth, $3.50.

Life on the Mississippi.—8vo, 624 pages; and over 300 illustrations. Sheep, $4.25; cloth, $3.50.

Innocents Abroad; or, The New Pilgrim's Progress. Sheep, $4.00; cloth, $3.50.

Roughing It.—600 pages; 300 illustrations. Sheep, $4.00; cloth, $3.50.

Sketches, Old and New.—320 pages; 122 illustrations. Sheep, $3.50; cloth, $3.00.

Adventures of Tom Sawyer.—150 engravings; 275 pages. Sheep, $3.25; cloth, $2.75.

The Gilded Age.—576 pages; 212 illustrations. Sheep, $4.00; cloth, $3.50.

A Tramp Abroad. Mark Twain in Europe.—A Companion Volume to "Innocents Abroad." 631 pages. Sheep, $4.00; cloth, $3.50.

THE WAR SERIES.

The Genesis of the Civil War.—The Story of Sumter, by Major-General S. W. Crawford, A. M., M. D., LL. D. Illustrated with steel and wood engravings and fac-similes of celebrated letters. 8vo, uniform with Grant's Memoirs. Full morocco, $8.00; half morocco, $5.50; sheep, $4.25; cloth, $3.50.

Personal Memoirs of General Grant.—Illustrations and maps, etc. 2 vols.; 8vo. Half morocco, per set, $11.00; sheep, per set, $9.00; cloth, per set, $7.00. A few sets in full Turkey morocco and tree calf for sale at special low prices.

Personal Memoirs of General Sherman.—With appendix by Hon. James G. Blaine. Illustrated; 2 vols.; 8vo, uniform with Grant's Memoirs. Half morocco, per set, $8.50; sheep, per set, 7.00; cloth, per set, $5.00. Cheap edition, in one large volume, cloth binding, $2.00.

Standard Publications of C. L. Webster & Co.

Personal Memoirs of General Sheridan.—Illustrated with steel portraits and woodcuts; 26 maps; 2 vols.; 8vo, uniform with Grant's Memoirs. Half morocco, per set, $10.00; sheep, per set, $8.00; cloth, per set, $6.00. A few sets in full Turkey morocco and tree calf to be disposed of at very low figures. Cheap edition, in one large volume, cloth binding, $2.00.

McClellan's Own Story.—With illustrations from sketches drawn on the field of battle by A. R. Waud, the Great War Artist. 8vo, uniform with Grant's Memoirs. Full morocco, $9.00; half morocco, $6.00; sheep, $4.75; cloth, $3.75.

Memoirs of John A. Dahlgren.—Rear-Admiral United States Navy. By his widow, Madeleine Vinton Dahlgren. A large octavo volume of 660 pages, with steel portrait, maps, and illustrations. Cloth, $3.00.

Reminiscences of Winfield Scott Hancock—By his wife. Illustrated; steel portraits of General and Mrs. Hancock; 8vo, uniform with Grant's Memoirs. Full morocco, $5.00; half morocco, $4.00 sheep, $3.50; cloth, $2.75.

Tenting on the Plains.—With the Life of General Custer. By Mrs. E. B. Custer. Illustrated; 8vo, uniform with Grant's Memoirs. Full morocco, $7.00; half morocco, $5.50; sheep, $4.25; cloth, $3.50.

Portrait of General Sherman.—A magnificent line etching on copper; size 19x24 inches: by the celebrated artist, Charles B. Hall. $2.00. (Special prices on quantities.)

The Great War Library.—Consisting of the best editions of the foregoing seven publications (Grant, Sheridan, Sherman, Hancock, McClellan, Custer and Crawford). Ten volumes in a box; uniform in style and binding. Half morocco, $50.00; sheep, $40.00; cloth, $30.00.

OTHER BIOGRAPHICAL WORKS.

Life of Jane Welsh Carlyle.—By Mrs. Alexander Ireland. With portrait and fac-simile letter; 8vo, 324 pages. Vellum cloth, gilt top, $1.75.

Life and Letters of Roscoe Conkling.—By Hon. Alfred R. Conkling, Ph. B., LL.D.; steel portrait and fac-similes of important letters to Conkling from Grant, Arthur, Garfield, etc. 8vo, over 700 pages. Half morocco, $5.50; full seal, $5.00; sheep, $4.00; cloth, $3.00.

Standard Publications of C. L. Webster & Co.

Life of Pope Leo XIII.—By Bernard O'Reilly, D. D., L. D. (Laval.) Written with the encouragement and blessing of His Holiness, the Pope. 8vo, 635 pages; colored and steel plates, and full-page illustrations. Half morocco, $6.00; half Russia, $5.00; cloth, gilt edges, $3.75.

Distinguished American Lawyers.—With their Struggles and Triumphs in the Forum. Containing an elegantly engraved portrait, autograph and biography of each subject, embracing the professional work and the public career of those called to serve their country. By Henry W. Scott. Introduction by Hon. John J. Ingalls. A large royal octavo volume of 716 pages, with 62 portraits of the most eminent lawyers. Sheep, $4.25; cloth, $3.50.

FICTION AND POETRY.

Dan Beard. Moonblight and Six Feet of Romance.—Octavo, 250 pages, fully illustrated. This story we believe will take rank with "Looking Backward." It treats of some of the great social problems of the day in a novel, powerful, and intensely interesting manner. The hero becomes strangely endowed with the power of seeing people in their true light. It is needless to say that this power proves both a curse and a blessing, and leads to many and strange adventures. Mr. Beard's reputation as an artist is world-wide, and the numerous illustrations he provides for this book powerfully portray the spirit of the text. Cloth, ink and gold stamps, $1.00.

Matt Crim. In Beaver Cove and Elsewhere.—Octavo, about 350 pages, illustrated.

PRESS OPINIONS.

"A writer who has quickly won wide recognition by short stories of exceptional power."—*New York Independent.*
"Her stories bear the stamp of genius."—*St. Paul Globe.*

This volume contains all of Miss Crim's most famous short stories. These stories have received the highest praise from eminent critics and prominent literary journals, and have given Miss Crim a position among the leading lady writers of America. Cloth, handsomely stamped, $1.00.

Standard Publications of C. L. Webster & Co.

Matt Crim. Adventures of a Fair Rebel.—12mo, 325 pages. A story that is sure to be eagerly sought after by Miss Crim's many admirers, North and South.

PRESS OPINION.

"It is a love story of unusual sweetness, pathos and candor."—*Christian Union.*

Stamped cloth, $1.00; paper covers, 50 cents.

Elisabeth Cavazza. Don Finimondone: Calabrian Sketches.—In *Fiction, Fact, and Fancy Series.* The publishers feel safe in saying that few American authors have so completely captured the Italian spirit as Mrs. Cavazza has done in these stories of Italian life among the lowly. Stamped cloth, gilt titles, 75 cents.

George R. Sims. Tinkletop's Crime, and eighteen other short stories, by this noted English novelist. 12mo, 316 pages. Cloth, $1.00; paper covers, 50 cents.

Leo Tolstoi. Ivan the Fool, and Other Stories.—12mo, 175 pages. Translated direct from the Russian by Count Norraikow, with illustrations by the celebrated Russian artist, Gribayédoff. 12mo. Cloth, $1.00.

Leo Tolstoi. Life IS Worth Living, and Other Stories.—12mo, 230 pages. Translated direct from the Russian by Count Norraikow. This work, unlike some of his later writings, shows the great Russian at his best. The stories are pure, simple and powerful, intensely interesting as mere creations of fancy, but, like all Tolstoi's works, written for a purpose, and containing abundant food for earnest reflection. Cloth, ink and gold stamps, $1.00.

Edgar Janes Bliss. The Peril of Oliver Sargent.—12mo. Cloth, $1.00; paper covers, 50 cents.

Walt Whitman. Selected Poems.—In *Fiction, Fact, and Fancy Series.* Edited by Arthur Stedman. This volume contains the best and most popular of Walt Whitman's poetical writings. The selections were made and the book is published by special permission of the author.

PRESS OPINION.

"That in Walt Whitman which is virile and bardic, lyrically fresh and sweet, or epically grand and elemental, will be preserved to the edification of young men and maidens, as well as of maturer folks.—*Hartford Courant.*

Stamped cloth, gilt titles, 75 cents.

Standard Publications of C. L. Webster & Co.

Irving Bacheller. The Master of Silence: A Romance.—In *Fiction, Fact, and Fancy Series*. Mr. Bacheller's first serious effort in fiction will be looked for with interest by those familiar with his poems and stories in the magazines. Stamped cloth, gilt titles, 75 cents.

William Sharp. Flower o' the Vine: Romantic Ballads and Sospiri di Roma.—Large 12mo, of about 200 pages. This volume contains the poems in Mr. Sharp's latest books of verse, now entirely out of print. His collaboration with Blanche Willis Howard in the novel "A Fellowe and His Wife," has made his name familiar to American readers. As one of the most popular of the younger English poets, we anticipate an equal success in America for "Flower o' the Vine," for which Mr. Thomas A. Janvier has prepared an Introduction. Handsomely bound, uniform with Aldrich's "Sisters' Tragedy" and Cora Fabbri's "Lyrics." Cloth, $1.50.

S. L. M. Byers. The Happy Isles, and Other Poems.—Small 12mo. Cloth binding, $1.00.

MISCELLANEOUS.

Concise Cyclopedia of Religious Knowledge.—Biblical, Biographical, Theological, Historical and Practical; edited by Rev. E. B. Sanford, M. A., assisted by over 30 of the most eminent religious scholars in the country. 1 vol.; royal 8vo, nearly 1,000 double-column pages. Half morocco, $6.00; sheep, $5.00; cloth, $3.50.

Yale Lectures on Preaching, and other Writings by Rev. Nathaniel Burton, D. D.; edited by Richard E. Burton. 8vo, 640 pages; steel portrait. Cloth, $3.75.

Legends and Myths of Hawaii.—By the late King Kalakaua; two steel portraits and 25 other illustrations. 8vo, 530 pages. Cloth, $3.00.

The Diversions of a Diplomat in Turkey.—By the late Hon. S. S. Cox. 8vo, 685 pages; profusely illustrated. Half morocco, $6.00; sheep, $4.75; cloth, $3.75.

Standard Publications of C. L. Webster & Co.

Inside the White House in War Times.—By W. O. Stoddard, one of Lincoln's Private Secretaries. 12mo, 244 pages. Cloth, $1.00.

My Life with Stanley's Rear Guard.—By Herbert Ward, one of the Captains of Stanley's Rear Guard; includes Mr Ward's Reply to H. M. Stanley. 12mo. Cloth, $1.00; paper covers, 50 cents.

Physical Beauty: How to Obtain and How to Preserve It, by Annie Jenness Miller; including chapters on Hygiene, Foods, Sleep, Bodily Expression, the Skin, the Eyes, the Teeth, the Hair, Dress, the Cultivation of Individuality, etc., etc. An octavo volume of about 300 pages. Cloth, $2.00.

The Table.—How to Buy Food, How to Cook It, and How to Serve It. 8vo, 500 pages, by A. Filippini, of Delmonico's; the only book ever endorsed by Delmonico; contains three menus for each day in the year, and over 1,500 original recipes, the most of which have been guarded as secrets by the *chefs* of Delmonico. Contains the simplest as well as the most elaborate recipes. Presentation edition in full seal Russia, $4.50; Kitchen edition in oil-cloth, $2.50.

One Hundred Ways of Cooking Eggs.—Mr. Filippini is probably the only man who can cook eggs in a hundred different ways, and this little book will be worth its price ten times over to any purchaser. 16mo, 128 pages. Cloth binding, ink and gold stamps, 50 cents.

Also, uniform with the above,

One Hundred Recipes for Cooking and Serving Fish.—This book contains only the best recipes, all of which have been tested by Mr. Filippini during 25 years' experience with the Delmonicos. 16mo, 128 pages. Cloth binding, ink and gold stamps, 50 cents.

Hour-Glass Series.—By Daniel B. Lucas, LL. D., and J. Fairfax McLaughlin, LL. D. The first volume, which is now ready, contains a series of historical epitomes of national interest, with interesting sketches of such men as Henry Clay, Daniel O'Connell and Fisher Ames. Large 12mo. Cloth, $1.00.

Standard Publications of C. L. Webster & Co.

(SOLD BY SUBSCRIPTION ONLY.)

The Library of American Literature. 1607-1891. Compiled and edited by Edmund Clarence Stedman and Ellen Mackay Hutchinson. In eleven Large Octavo Volumes of over 500 pages each. Fifteen Full-Page Portraits in each Volume, many of which are Rare and Valuable. Vol. XI. contains BIOGRAPHICAL NOTICES of all authors quoted, selections from recent literary productions, and an exhaustive topical index of the entire work.

PRESS OPINIONS.

These volumes are a substantial addition to popular literature, and make, as they profess to do, a library of our best American reading for the people at large. —*The Atlantic Monthly*, Boston.

It not only makes the reader well acquainted with the progress of American literature, but shows him its relation to the life of the people with a vividness and accuracy which no historian has yet attempted.—*New York Tribune.*

Earnest gratitude is due to the poet-critic and the charming lyrist whose combined studies have produced so valuable a work.—*The Critic*, New York.

No popular review, on anything like an appropriate scale, has before been made of our national literature; for, though in its beginning it was studiously modeled on the parent source, it has grown to be as distinctly national as any other phase of American development.—*San Francisco Argonaut.*

It is both a pleasure and a privilege to taste of this literary feast, a mental feast, unparalleled in its completeness and excellence.—*North American Review.*

In Cloth, $3.00 per volume; sheep, $4.00 per volume; half Turkey morocco, gilt top, cut edges, also marbled edges, $5.00 per volume; half Levant crushed, $7.00 per volume.

www.ingramcontent.com/pod-product-compliance
Lightning Source LLC
Chambersburg PA
CBHW031827230426
43669CB00009B/1247